KING DESIGNS

# Paws For Thought

Edited
By
ADAM KING

PUBLISHING

First published in Great Britain in 1997 by
**KING DESIGNS**
56 Bringhurst, Orton Goldhay,
Peterborough, PE2 5RT.

British Library Cataloguing in Publication Data.
A catalogue record for this book is available from the British Library.

Cover Design by Robert Gautreaux

Printed and Bound in Great Britain by
Parrot Print Ltd
Unit 1 Park Farm Workshops,
Wood Lane, Ramsey,
Cambridgeshire, PE17 1XF.

Softback ISBN - 1 901349 04 7
Hardback ISBN - 1 901349 05 5

# Beachwood Boarding Kennels
# & Canine Relocation Centre

**Hartland - Bideford**
**North Devon - EX39 6HF**

## DONATIONS APPEAL

The Canine Relocation Centre, although a small centre, has rehomed over a thousand dogs since we were founded in February, 1993. Because we are small, we do, unfortunately struggle for funding. We rehouse for the RSPCA as well as the general public. We specialise in gundog breeds and G.S.D. which, being dominant dogs that cannot be rehomed to the general public, are saved by being rehomed to the Civilian Police Force and Military Police for search and protection work.

The C.R.C. is funded solely by public donation.
Fund-raisers, voluntary help, blankets & other dog related items always required.
Money is needed for vaccinations, neutering, feed bills, vet bills, accessories etc....
Donations are gratefully accepted.  Cheques payable to C.R.C.

**Tel. Pete on**
**(01237) 441799**

*(10% profits from this book have been donated to the centre.)*

# *Foreword*

That loveable canine companion has often been called man's best friend, and this cannot be more apparent than in this anthology. *Paws For Thought* looks into the companionship and loyalty that dogs express towards humans, and it is clear that this special bond is an unbreakable one. The poets included take a look at the relationship between the dog and their owners (often the other way around *!*), expressing a diverse range of emotions ranging from: affection; sorrow; humour and fond memories. *Paws For Thought* was a joy to edit, and a delight to read for all dog lovers.

Many thanks to the publishers who supported us through publicity - *Your Dog, Dogs Today, Dogs Monthly*.

Adam King
Editor

# *Contents*

# Polly The Pain

A brindle / white Boston from her ears to her toes,
With a short crooked tail and a squashed up nose.
Popping out eyes and a mouth ear to ear,
Lively and funny, an adorable dear.

Just mention a walk and she's off like a shot,
Runs around in circles, then sits panting and hot.
Kneels by the fire - not all dogs do that,
Starts nodding off and rolls out flat.

She snores like a tug-boat over-powering the telly,
Grins and squirms with delight if you tickle her belly.
Chews up her toys and plays till all hours,
A loveable friend and we're glad that she's ours.

*G. H. P.*

# Anno Domini

They sat together on the lawn one day in early spring,
A Tabby cat, a Poodle dog with one small rubber ring.
"Please, Pussy Cat" the Poodle said, "please come and play with me"
The Tabby smiled and shook her head "I'm very old, you see".

"Say, Pussy Cat, how old are you?" the Poodle did enquire.
"I am so old that at my age most normal cats expire".
"Pray just how old is this great age to which no cat survives?"
The cat just nodded sleepily and said she'd had nine lives.

"But you" she added with a smile "are only just a pup".
You must not think of growing old when you have scarce grown up.
Your youth still lies before you, your life has just begun,
You do not mind when humans shout, for you, you see, can run".

"Yes I can bounce and bark and play and toss this ring about,
And what care I if humans scold or point at me and shout?
For I am young and in this world there's nothing that I dread"
At this the cat smiled knowingly and shook her ageing head.

"There was a time when I could run the way you do today,
When I could chase a cotton reel or catch a mouse at play,
Those days are past and now I fear I only sit and dream
Of all the things that used to be or things that might have been".

"But tell me" said the Poodle as she licked a dainty paw,
"You must know many stories that I've never heard before"
"So many" said the Tabby "it would take five solid years
To tell them all, and some so sad you'd find yourself in tears".

"For growing old is very sad, your friends all pass away
And you are left to wait your turn which may come any day".
And at this thought she gave a sigh and then a weary yawn,
The dog then left her with her dreams, alone upon the lawn.

*Anna P. Smith*

# In Memory Of

The years rushed by so quickly
It shouldn't be that way
It seems like only yesterday
When she came here to stay.

She brought me love and warmth and hope
She gave me all she had
She made me laugh when I was down
And smile when I was sad.

We didn't have to say much
It was there and understood
A friendship bonded from the start
I always knew it would.

But now the house is empty
And she's no longer there
I miss my dog, my Candy
My friend
Oh it's not fair!

*S. Elmes*

# The Dog's Home

The sound of cries and
       frightened barks.
The dogs are found on
       streets and parks.
Pitiful creatures, no food
       for days.
Fur falling out, they're
       typical strays.
Puppies too young to have
       left their mum.
Cuddled together, no time
       for fun.
Rottweillers, Dobremans, Boxers
       and Pugs.
Sitting and staring, no
       kisses or hugs.
Crossbreeds and pedigrees
       all cast aside.
Nowhere to run, to play
       or to hide.
The people come and
       stare through the bars.
Arriving by foot or travelling
       in cars.
A little puppy, catches
       someone's eyes.
It barks hopefully, then
       whimpers and cries.
All they want is for someone
       to care.
Food and love and a home
       to share.

Away from the noise
       and this awful smell
To live in peace
       instead of hell.

*C. A. Saberton*

# Harry

To Mummy Love Jo *x x x x*

It was last winter, on a Wednesday, I think,
My mum's face was all rosy, her cheeks were bright pink!
She oozed with excitement, and was happy as could be
For today was the day she would buy her puppy!

We climbed in the car, and to Farnham we went
(Yes, this is what buying a standard poodle meant)
It was nothing but hassle all the way there
We got lost four times, but mum didn't care.

We arrived at two instead of ten
(Glad I'm not doing this again!)
As we walked in the house, this little black ball
Came bounding over and jumped on us all.

"This is Flash Harry, we like him the best"
And a piece of white fluff stood out on his chest.
He looked kind of cute, with that white piece of hair
Which we were told, shouldn't have been there!

And when the breeder bent down to cover it up,
My mum fell in love with this little black pup.

So we put him in the car, and took him home,
And ten months later, you should see how he's grown.
Now he looks more like a horse
But who still loves him, Mum of course!

*Jo Murray*

# Dumped On The Motorway

To a barren hillside
Committed
I am crouching, poised for flight.
I watch, take stock,
Dare not go back

To the road that bayed for my blood,
From which I fled.  This hunk of rock
This heavyweight,
I have signed with my scent
For my own.  Why then

Do I cower, weak as a puppy
Kicked by a careless boot?
By day

I scavenge, I forage
In witless sorties,
Nuzzling litter
Searching for bones;
I drink
From a shallow basin of clay,
Warm my coat
On a ragged sleeve of the sun;

I fear the pain.
It is the pain of hunger
It will not pass away,

Fear too
The dry grey smell of snow,
The brutal snap
Of winter's frigid jaws and fangs of ice.

I have a choice.

I can throw in my lot
With the vagabonds,
Become a nameless cur,

Or tail-struck make tracks
For the lap of the gods,
Find me another god.  I am a dog

Who has harmed neither man nor fellow-beast,
And I would not bite
The hand stretched out -

A stranger's hand,
To bless and feed.

*Kathleen Norcross*

# The Breeders Prayer

Good evening dear lord, on this clear bright night,
I've a favour to ask if you're listening tonight.
Remember the puppy who was born to small?
I was sure he would die and him to heaven you'd call.
Then in your wisdom you gave him his life,
Each day he grew stronger, overcoming his strife.
Just look at him now! He's handsome and bold,
And as happy and healthy as any ten week old.

There was a lady who called at my house today,
She fell in love with that puppy and took him away.
Though I know in my heart that she will be kind,
it isn't that which is on my mind.
You see she's never owned a dog before,
And I know too well the trouble it may cause.
So the favour I'm asking, if you'd be so good,
Is keep an eye on them both and help if you could.
Show them the way into each others heart,
And teach them to love right from the start.
Show them understanding and lord as a must,
Let from the beginning in each other be trust.

*Jackie Muir*

# My Dear Old Friend

I remember you as a puppy
All ears and skinny legs
With a crinkle-cut nose
Wobbling around and falling down
My dear old friend.

As you grew bigger
You were much stronger
And pulled me off my feet
But I did not mind
You silly old dog.

You became my friend
As we both matured
We loved to go walks
And play in the park
When you were much fitter.

You were always there
When I came home
With your stumpy tail wagging
And those big sad eyes
But, oh dear, do not shake your head!

Now my friend, as you know
I have moved on in life
You had to stay where you know best
Because you would be lost
As I am now, without you
My Dear Old Friend.
Dedicated to Bruno

*Diane Simpson*

# Daisy

10 years of faithful service
we used to walk and play.

10 years of faithful service
I am now lost and afraid.

10 years of faithful service
I am now classed as a stray.

10 years of faithful service
perhaps a fine is too much to pay.

10 years of faithful service
I sit in this kennel and pray.

10 years of faithful service
today is the seventh day.

10 years of faithful service
am I really too old and grey.

10 years of faithful service
someone is coming my way.

10 years of faithful service
I feel myself drift away.

10 years of faithful service
I am no longer afraid.

*Elizabeth Colley*

# Our German Shepherd Pup

I'm a happy little puppy name of Ross
When I got home I thought I'd be the boss
But that's not how it goes
They sometimes smack my nose
And when I'm really naughty they are cross.

I love this home in which I've come to stay
Where I only have to eat and sleep and play
And all that seems to matter
Is to listen to them natter
About the antics I get up to every day.

I shall protect my home and hearth in every way
For I am growing bigger, bigger, bigger every day
And I'll love them to the end
As I know I'm their best friend
Because of what they do and what they say.

*Joan Richards*

# Walking With Wolves

Sometimes when I cannot sleep,
I take his lead and enter night,
and climb the hill behind the house,
to where the daylight dog,
of fawning ways and comfy bed
does not exist.
there, he seems to glide
with lupine grace
along the shrouded paths,
and I, with a deep primeval fear,
sense other gliding figures near.
And when the crest is reached,
he lifts his shaggy head,
and gives one long mournful cry,
and fellow dogs nearby,
in barns and fire-warmed rooms,
find stirring in their ancestral genes,
a memory as old as time,
and so their cries answer him.
Then, he comes, and licks my hand,
and there against the moonlight sky,
I see freedom burning in his eyes,
and I feel humble, that he walks with me.

*Pat Hancock*

# Kim

You were a joy my close companion, sweet and loyal and true
And my life was so much happier for the time I spent with you.

Your wagging tail and happy grin no longer there at each days end,
I still miss your clumsy greeting, my trusted brown eyed friend.

You tried so hard to stay with me for just a little longer,
You were so tired although you tried to be a little stronger.

I didn't know that evening would begin your final sleep
But all those precious times we shared are treasures I can keep.

I just wish I could have held you, touched your silky head once more
But God put his arms around you and between us closed the door.

you were my good companion mischievous much loved too
And my life was full of laughter in the time I spent with you.

The memories you left for me will last my whole life through
And until we meet again my friend goodnight and God bless you.

*Lynn Taylor*

## Dandie Rap

My name is 'Celandine', after the flower
I'm a brave wee lass never known to cower
I love to go to Ringcraft at Littlewick Green
Where I'm the most mischievous Dandie Dinmont they've ever seen!
Going in the show ring never gets up my nose -
I love to drag Mum around the shows
My 'other' life is equally good
And I do everything a Dandie should
I kill the rats by shaking them twice
And mice die quicker so that is nice
I swim in the river whenever I can
It cools me better than any car fan!
I chase the fisherman's rods and floats
And flash my top-knot at passing boats
With garden toads I love to play
Making them squeak.... and spit poison spray.
That can make me feel quite sick
But I get better awfully quick.
Other creatures aren't so kind
I got bitten by an adder and it blew my mind!
I've even entered a Terrier race
But I couldn't match the Jack Russell's pace.
I do so much, I have great dreams
Of adventures, shows and peppermint creams
So when I'm stuck in my cage at 'Crufts'
Please don't think that a Dandie life is tough.
I'm one of many who have such fun
Life isn't just the cards we won.

*'Celandine' - Westwell Cupid's Love - Aged 4*
*& Stephanie Fitt*

# Little Black-Eyed Susie

We called her black spot
The day she was born;
A little fat bulldoggy pup.
Her black spot turned brown
Her face wrinkled and frowned
Her velvet ears shaped like a rose
With black eyes, black lips and black nose.

Her fat wrinkled face smiled at us with glee.
Her black eyes would twinkle and shine.
She'd snuggle up close and lick at my face
She'd snuffle and then softly whine
As the love in her eyes said 'Hug me'
While she wriggled so pleased to be mine.

But the years took their toll
And no longer we'd stroll
As her legs and her heart grew tired.
Her bright eyes turned dim
The love shone within
From that little fat bulldog of mine.

She was twelve years of age
And become frail and old
As the tumour inside of her grew.
The end, it had come
And no more could I do
For my little fat bulldog called Sue.

We'll never forget you, Susie.
We loved you through all of those years
And though you're not with us
We love you still
And for ever and always, we will.

**Mary Dixon**

# It's a Dogs Life

One often hears it said, by the human race today
"Isn't it a dogs life", when things don't go their way
Do they know what they are saying, they do not, you can be sure
For I am talking from experience, so I will tell you more
I wake up in the morning, and rise up from my bed
Then stroll around the garden, until breakfast I am fed
After that I have a walk, which may be long or short
Depending on the weather, should it rain, I won't get caught
When I get back my coat is brushed, I am made to look quite smart
Is this then that dogs life, that was mentioned at the start
I then find myself a quiet spot, and settle down to sleep
For there will be another walk quite soon, an appointment I must keep
Sometimes in the car I go, and walk around a wood
It appears it is the thing to do, they say it does me good
Then home once more, its time by then, to be served up with my tea
This of course is brought to me, they always wait on me
Another snooze, and then we're off, to stroll around once more
That ends the day with nowt to do, but lay around and snore
So when they say they are led a dogs life, and as they weep and wail
There is one thing that is quite certain, that dog is no **Airedale**.

*S. C. Wiggins*

# When You Looked At Me

When you looked at me with your gentle eye,
I'm so sorry I had to say goodbye.
All those years we ran and played.
They were in your happier days
Then you grew old and could hardly run,
But you still tried to have your fun,
Like our last walk in the park,
And how we played in the dark,
Me not wanting dawn to come
You not knowing it would be your last one.
Your graceful head fell to the ground,
Your weak body was crippled and bound.
You tried to stand, but nothing was left
Then you breathed your final breath,
I stayed with you till the end
To say goodbye, faithful friend.

*Holly Mason*

# Sally

We'd definitely decided
Not to have another dog.
We convinced ourselves
We were too old
The final trauma was too great
We'd not be 'tied' again.

We took a holiday abroad
We went to all those places
Where dogs are not allowed;
Walked all those beaches
Where they're banned
Throughout the summer.

I tried to like my tidy home -
No hairs, no muddy prints, no bones:
But all to no avail.
I sneaked down to the local Pound
Just to have a look -
And there she was.

Pressed against the bars,
Skinny, black and longing for a home.
Oh the joy of muddy paws and hairy floors
The delight of holidays for three
Long country walks and most of all -
Her loving company.

*Pamela May*

# From Max

I am a little Lowchen.
I'm always full of fun.
Just listen for a minute
I'll tell you what I've done
I saw this great big bag of crisps
Standing in the corner there
Just waiting to be eaten up,
And there was no-one else to share
My mistress came in through the door
She said "That's all I've got"
I looked at her with big brown eyes
Which said "Too late I ate the lot"
My mistress is called Mandy
She goes to work all day
She gives me lots of cuddles
When she comes back home to stay
I have a friend called Simon
A Border Collie pup
I see him when my doggie minder
Comes to pick me up.
She teaches me to sit and stay
And takes me walkies, every day
I have to say 'Bye Bye' now
My eyes are getting red
So here's a big wet sloppy kiss
Before I go to bed.

*Love From Max*
Kennal Name "Super Trouper"

## *Ruby True*

# Little And Large

Boris is a Rottweiler plagued by Jock
Who's a Westie I 'rescued' from a bad pet shop
Boris is three years and Jock is one
So you can imagine we have great fun
Boris is so gentle - Jock is cocky
So the relationship at first was a little rocky
Jock bites Boris's ears and pulls his jowls
Boris loves it all and never growls
Boris has never chewed or torn
But Jock is digging up the lawn
Another crime I have to pardon -
More plants indoors than in the garden
I return from work to give them both a hug
To find geraniums and daises indoors on the rug
Jock is supposed to be white but he's always black
Forever rolling in cow-pats on his back
But he's so cute he makes you laugh
He spends more time than I do in the bath
Boris the Rottweiler - the supposedly 'dangerous' one
Who Jock is forever biting on the bum
To make him chase him round the tree
The pair of them are a sight to see
They're the best of friends and love one another
But Jock thinks he is Boris's brother
He's afraid of nothing of any size
And will stare a bullock in the eyes
As remarked to me by the local tiler
He's a Westie who thinks he's a big Rottweiler!

*Rose Horscroft*

# Solace

There was a fey Pointer called Lace,
Who took off with indecent haste.
The bellows of justified fury,
Could be heard by a stone deaf jury.
When eventually all but cornered,
There was nothing to do but as ordered.
She sat in a veritable dither,
And came when a finger called her hither.
Not a word itself was spoken,
The spell must not be broken.

The feather adorning her soft quivering mouth,
Was snatched and flung precipitously South.
Two hands to her neck descended,
Was the punishment to be amended?
Two glaring, burning, much loved eyes,
Bored relentlingly with no guise.
A deep and shaking breath was taken,
Two ears were roughly pulled and shaken.
'You imp of Satan, you bloody toad,
I'll send you off up the road.
If you chase one more chicken,
It's the road to North Devon you'll be picking.
You knew at once you were in the wrong,
Or I shouldn't have run after you so long.
Nor run and run so fast away,
If you were right, it's not your way.
Just you once more leap that coop,
I'll put you through the blasted hoop.
Oh dear, dear me, Lace what a muddle,
Come here and we'll have a cuddle'.

### *Anne C. Terrell*

# A Man's Best Friend

Choosing a friend can be a worry
Not an easy thing to do
A decision you can't make in a hurry
As it can mean a lot to you.

You could do worse than choose a dog
To be your friend for life
He will stay with you through life's hard slog
And share your pain and strife.

A truly loyal friend he'll be
Of that there is no doubt
Right by your side for all to see
Whether your indoors or out.

He will love being taken for a walk
Or just down to the shops
You do not even have to talk
He'll walk with you 'till he drops.

He wont complain, or moan, or fuss
He's just happy that you're there
And he will join you in the car or bus
Or just lie there by your chair.

You'll always get a welcome whenever you return
A happy yelp, a wagging tail
From this loving friend you cannot spurn
Nor must you ever fail.

What does he ask for? not a lot
Some kindness, love, and care
So give your true friend all you've got
And for you he's always there.

*Nicola McLeod*

# The Puppy

FOR SNOOKIE AND EVERYONE WHO HELPED IN HER RESCUE,
CARE AND SURVIVAL

'A fortnight old,' the vet said
'Too young to leave her mum'.
'But mum's home was a cold dark shed
My new home's always warm.
No fights for food with litter mates
I'm never hungry now.
Please let me stay
I'm not too young
I promise to be good'.


'She's small and weak, she may not live.
You know you'll have a fight;
Feed her good rich milky food
To help her build up strength'.
'So they bottle fed me day and night
And lavished me with love.
My life was precious
I see now
I am a lucky girl'.

'That's all nearly twelve years past,
I have a blessed life.
With walks in Wales and holidays
In all parts of these Isles.
From Devon's fields
To Scotland's hills
And Yorkshire's moors and Dales
I've walked and barked and swum
And played with Ringo,
My best friend'.

**Lynne Roberts**

# They Called Him The Champion

Champion was his name, racing his game
A real Champ, victorious
With a smile a mile wide
You could feel his pride, when his owner
Held the prize aloft for all to see, and

Said to the ones who coveted his throne
"He'll always be first dog home.  Can you all see
What this King of dogs means to me
My money-spinner, see me, proud owner of the winner?".

Until he came in third.  The word
Soon buzzed around the track
He's lost his hold, he'll not be back
He's knackered, leg's gone, see it's three
He's walking on.  Mark my words he's done
That's the last you'll see of The Champion".

A van turned off a country track
And big, beseeching eyes looked back
Bred in captivity he'd never roamed
Muzzled up away from home
No bowl, no bed, just mangled limb and jangled head.

Crack! he heard a huntsman's gun
His instincts told him he must run, because everything's
Running, running where?  Where's the hare?  He rested
Weary head on throbbing leg, wasn't he The Champion?

*Joan V. Park*

29

# Thoughts Of a Dog

We come in all shapes, some large, some small
Long hair and short hair, one none at all.

Barking ones, silent ones, we all have our ways
But we must inform people that one of these days

You must wake to the fact that all is not well
For some of us dogs, life can be just pure hell

You are the masters, the rulers of all
And will shout and kick if there's mess in the hall

We dogs cannot speak or explain how it feels
To be thrown outside to lick bruises and weal's

So I chew a chair leg, you don't think it's funny
You blame me again, those chairs, they cost money

Understand I'm alive, I have a body and brain
I am what you made me, please don't shout again

You tell me I'm lucky to be living with you
When I was a pup I believed all that too

You took me away from my friends and my mum
I loved all your cuddles and rubs on my tum

But grow up I did, so did you think ahead,
That one day I could question the things that you said?

You say I'm a burden, a nuisance to you
Yet still in my way I love all that you do

When all your friends go and you're left quite alone
I am still here, I even give you my bone

I won't let you down like all your friends can
I don't think that way, it's just how I am

So perhaps all you people who are planning a pet
Could glance at these words, and never forget

We breathe, we're alive, we'll come when you call
So please treat us right, or don't have us at all..

*Brian G. Clarke*

# Sanctuary

I'm working at a sanctuary and seeing every day
Creatures sad and lonely but I've rarely time for play
I feed them, groom and clean them - how I wish there was a way
To find good homes for them.

The jetsam of divorce and death, of cruelty and neglect
The puppy who outgrew the flat - Well, what did they expect?
Dogs strayed and old, unwanted pets so please do not reject
My plea to help them.

We'd like to have more money, it could buy them little treats
Like toys to fill their empty days (for many, empty weeks)
But its not their first priority, for what they really seek's
Someone to love them.

Think, if you'd like an animal, if you could give a home
To a waiting one that otherwise would spend his days alone
There are many thousands shut away - your aid could help atone
For what we've done to them.

So come up to the sanctuary, its open every week
And you may find the friend you want, and he the love he seeks
For there are some happy endings when good dogs and owners meet
Are you one of them?

*Lorraine Phipps*

# The Lurcher

Do you remember days of yore,
And all that went before?
When King John decreed
That we where an elite breed.
We were symbols of status
And all true huntsman rated us.
If an peasant dared to disobey
It was a hanging offence right away.

Do you remember when
It was only landed gentlemen
Were allowed a hound
So graceful and so sound?
When did it all go wrong?
When did we not belong?
Misconceptions abound
About having us around.
We are loving and kind.
And no where would you find.
A more faithful friend
On whom you can depend.

We only need half hours run
And a little bit of fun.
So why are we hounds
Filing the compounds?
Every dog has its day
So they say.
Will ours ever return?
Will we have the love that we yearn?
Next time, don't turn away
From another skinny stray.
And give us a chance.

*Sue Jewell*

# Molly

Trimmed to perfection,
with show-dog features,
her adult beauty
emerges from the puppy coat.

Painted lady from fur-lined bear cub,
balanced markings,
neat black boots,
badger-head with white-brilliant stripe,

The blue roan spaniel
sheds her baby image
to become the promised first-born
of her handsome parents.

*Wendy Elson*

# All In a Dog's Day

It's a dogs life they say, but that's all right
My mistress always treats me right
She's given me a loving home
And from its warmth I'll never roam

I like a bone when I'm at home
And bury them in the garden
I buried a dozen and then some,
But can't recall where I put em!

My mistress hangs the washing on the line
And I toss my ball and have a great time
But she gets cross and it's a pain
She does the washing all over again

At Christmas time its really a joy
My mistress buys me a brand new toy
I chase it round the house with glee
And sometimes knock over the Christmas tree

When my mistress is fast asleep
Into her bedroom I do creep
I pull off the warm bedclothes
And nudge her awake with my cold wet nose

I love to run in the fields and play
With doggy friends all the day
My mistress comes too dressed in boots and Mac
And washes my paws when we get back

*Avril Coates*

36

# The Dog Star

I taught you all you know, you cur - I made you what you are
I sheltered you, I gave you food, I thought you'd be a star.
Now I'm dog-tired and you're dog-eared and we're both wondering why
I dogged your every moment, never let a sleeping dog lie.
You looked a real dog's dinner when we walked into that ring,
"Doggone" I heard somebody say "result's a foregone thing".
A man in a dog-collar was watching from behind -
He didn't seem to know that dogs have one thing on their mind.
Dog "Daisy" and Dog "Rose" were trotting primly in your wake
The dogsbody in charge should have discovered their mistake.
You lept into the fray, the dog lead flew out from my grasp,
The dog judge screamed and dropped her bag, the vicar gave a gasp.
You tried it on with "Daisy" first and then you switched to "Rose" -
A blare came from the tannoy "Get that Dog Out!    OUT HE GOES".
I dragged you off, my head hung low, a true hang-dog expression,
You didn't care what havoc was the cause of my depression.
I couldn't face that scene again, lie doggo you ingrate -
It's dog-eat-dog from now on pal, no dinner on your plate.
No hot-dog, dog-fish, dog-meat, chow, a very meagre diet,
I'll show you who's the boss, 'cos I'm the idiot who'll buy it.

This is all simply doggerel, all rubbish that is true,
For you're my dog, this man's best friend;  I'll keep you 'cos you're
you.
So wag your tail, sleep by the fire and stay the way you are.
No matter what folk think of you, you're Sirius, my Dog Star!!

*Gwen Stone*

# Spike

When you brought me to your home
Many years ago,
I chewed up all your furniture
You said I had to go.

But now I'm old, my joints are stiff
My running days are gone,
My face that once was handsome,
Is now ugly, grey and wrong.

Do the right thing by me mum,
And let me join my friends
To the place where dogs don't age,
And I can play again.

I know that it wont hurt me
I just go off to sleep,
I may be dead, but I'm not gone
My spirit you shall keep.

So when you get your new dog
And I think you should,
Don't compare him with me mum
He will be just as good.

### *Samantha Lakehal*

38

# Disguise

As I walk down the street
There's few people do pass by -
The strangers look at me
And all they see is my disguise.

Well my owner doesn't seem to notice,
And her friends that pop round all fuss me;
I know I'm big and broad:
But it's the complete opposite of my personality.

I watch all the people;
And see them fuss the pups who pass by,
And when I walk up to them,
I don't know why but they seem to get a big fright.

I don't mean to scare them,
All I want is a stroke and pat,
I always put on my best smile:
It's weird how they all seem to react just like cats!

Well maybe one day they won't run away;
And cross to the other side of the street.
I just hope one day that not everyone will be afraid;
'cause to be quiet honest once you get to know me I'm rather sweet.

Now they all say it's my breed -
Don't fuss me, don't love me;
Don't cuddle me at all.
But I just can't help it if I'm big, if I'm broad.

I know there's some doggies similar to me,
And are naughty and do tend to bite;
But why blame me, I always live by her rules;
Please don't be frightened even if I am a pitbull.

*Josephine Kirk*

# Leo

Mum, your tears are falling and your face is wet
You think you've lost your beloved pet
Dry your eyes, start anew
I'll never forget you - because you're you.

We've had our good times
We've had our bad
And I don't want you to feel sad
I've just moved on and I'll wait for you
No matter how long it takes, after what we've been through.

When you're walking and the stars are bright
Look to the Pet one and say - yes, that's right
I'll be up there playing like we used to do
Having a whale of a time - but still there with you.

So smile again and carry on
For because I'm not there with you - me and you are still one.

*Vanessa McLeod*

# Do Come On

I can't see why you take so long
It's always such a fuss
First the coat, then hat and gloves
Oh please do come on!

Count the biscuits fetch the lead
Let's put the harness on
Both paws in... good let's go
Oh please do come on!

Last the wellies.. now we're off
Check the key and walking stick
Round and through the garage door
Oh please do come on!

I'm eager to catch all the smells
And stop at every post
I hope we don't meet humans
Oh please do come on!

The scent is fresh I know it's bitch
I zig-zag frantically
She must be close.. yes there she is
Oh please do come on!

I know you'll stop and talk to Frank
You nearly always do
Our noses rub.. I think she cares
Lucy.. please do come on!

*Judith MacBeth*

# Domestication

The partnership we share is a bit of a fake
For one it's all give and the other all take
For the first is so able and so willing to please
That the other sits back and exploits what he sees.

He is used to protect and to keep out the crooks
He is used to gain money from the way that he looks
He finds travellers on mountains who get themselves lost
Some make him race for their pleasure, but at what cost?

For sniffing out quarry that I'd never find
For herding the flock
Or for guiding the blind
The tasks where my patience would quickly tire
He performs with a skill I can only admire.

He must behave in a way which suits our demands
To be there when he's called, and obey our commands
For this privilege he loves us whatever we do
He looks to us for company and enjoys is too
He's starved, forgotten, neglected and left to cope
But he comes back to man every time with fresh hope.

Can I be worth as much to him as he is to me?
Would he have been happier if wolves had been left free?
My equal partner, or so I pretend
But what I offer seems inadequate to deserve such a friend
Food, a warm bed and a safe place to live
He demands nothing more, and I have nothing more to give.

*Joanne Merry*

# Little Puppy

Little, lost puppy sitting under a tree.
Little, lost puppy looking up at me.
Little, sad puppy is all alone.
Little, sad puppy has no home.
Little, brave puppy once was a pet,
Who had toys and love, on that I will bet.
When along came a little kitten or bird,
And from then on never a kind word little puppy heard.
People had loved him, people had cared.
Not anymore was their love shared.
Little puppy, don't worry anymore.
Don't fret for,
I'll give you a home.
You'll no longer ever have to be alone,
Because I'll always be there,
To love you, to hug you, to kiss you, to care.

*Stephanie Upton (Aged 13)*

# Cuddles to Last a Lifetime

I cuddled you hard - so much to say
So few hours on your final day
Trying to let you see how I felt
Knowing the hand you were being dealt.
I know you were suffering I'm told it was best
To let you go swiftly and lay you to rest.
I wanted to keep you - I felt so bad
Knowing great trust was all that you had.
We did it for you I am told to believe
Then why am I finding it hard now to grieve?
All that I feel is pain and much guilt
Knowing we took the one that we built.
To stop you from suffering we took your life
And now into me is plunging the knife.
I still want to feel you and cuddle you tight
To hold you and kiss you and tell you goodnight.
I know that I'm selfish in feeling this way
And know that it's long since you had your best day.
Just wish I was certain you were ready to go
I wish there was some way of letting us know
But we had to watch you stumble and fall
We had to hold you and wait for your 'call'
Too long in coming - too much pain
For you - for us - though not the same.
You were so special so loving so dear
And inside our hearts you will always be near.
So I pray you'll forgive us and watch from above
And know when you left us you took ALL OUR LOVE.

*Sue Page*

# My Mutt

I fed his face twice daily, then scrubbed his feed bowl clean.
His coat I brushed until it shone, and nails I trimmed supreme.
I walked him three times every day in rain or snow or shine.
I trained him, fussed him, loved him and gave him 'quality time'.

When he was ill and needed help the vet I'd always call,
whose fees I'd always pay on time, be they large (or small?).
In Spring and Autumn when they came his fleas I zapped away,
then sprayed his bed and carpets to keep them all at bay.

His hairs I cleaned from chairs and mats, I washed him when he rolled.
I dried him off when he got wet so he did not catch cold.
I followed him with scoop and pail his whoopsies to dispose
(a job that made me sometimes wish I did not have a nose!!).

The tarter from his teeth I scraped, gum troubles to be eased.
If his rear he dragged along the mat, his anal glands I squeezed.
Worm tablets he got twice a year Tox. Canis to disperse,
To stop them affecting other dogs, or even something worse.

When we played ball, a game he loved, and after it he plunged
to bring it back with sheer delight, whose hand was it got 'gunged'?
Then on the days, when time allowed, I tried to watch T.V.
he'd bring his lead as if to say 'you should be watching me".

And of an evening when we took our usual country stroll,
To find and eat some rotting muck most often seemed his goal.
Now I loved that dog, I really did, to me he was most dear,
But at 3 a.m. my love was stretched when he got diarrhoea.

Now he has gone after fifteen years and left me here alone
with empty bowl and empty pail and half uneaten bone,
I sit in ponderence with time to spare and even have a drink.
You ask me if I'll miss that mutt -

**WHAT DO <u>YOU</u> BL . . . . WELL THINK! ! !**

*P. M. Brace*

# Greyhounds Can Make Great Pets

Rocky the greyhound is a perfect pet to me,
As devoted and intelligent as any dog could be,
I got him from the vet who was about to put him down,
Now his fame as a celebrity has spread from town to town,
He's had his picture in the paper with Sam my ginger car,
Lots of people came and told me they were so amazed at that.

He lives a life of luxury, his racing days are past,
Though he ran before I got him and was very, very fast,
A strained achillies tendon brought his racing to an end,
I walked into the vet's that day, acquired my faithful friend,
As I swept my hand along his glossy back I knew that I,
Just couldn't let that beautiful big black and white dog die.

So I took him home, that was the best thing I have ever done,
The years we've spent together have been wonderful, such fun,
He was fit again in no time and so seldom on a lead,
Running round in glorious freedom with exhilarating speed,
I've trained him and I've showed him, 'twas not difficult at all,
And he's won a few rosettes that proudly hang upon the wall.

It's a privilege to own him, I'm determined now that he,
Should be a walking advertisement, letting everybody see,
That greyhounds are worth saving, that they can make perfect pets,
Rocky's brought me only pleasure, absolutely no regrets,
But when I think of other greyhounds it reduces me to tears,
For far to many face destruction at the end of their careers.

And they are all just dogs like Rocky, with like him, the right to live,
Each deserves a caring owner for they've got so much to give,
They're such noble, patient creatures, how I love my Rocky so,
He's completely captivated me, I want the world to know,
That greyhounds can make GREAT pets, from now on you can be sure,
That to this breed I'm dedicated, trying to save the lives of more.

*Sheena Forrest*

# A Dog is For Life

A dog is just not for Christmas I heard people say,
So why then am I here in this strange place today,
I remember my first Christmas with my family so dear,
The laughter, kisses and hugs, oh its all so clear,
I grew so fast, they began to complain,
No time today to walk me in the rain,
At first my people always wanted me around,
Then they began to stare at me and frown,
He is too big, always in the way,
Get rid of him, he can no longer stay,
So here I am in the kennels, awaiting a new home,
I dream of someone to love and fields to roam,
If you are thinking of buying a dog,
Remember, we are not toys or wooden logs,
Are you sure you will have time for me in years to come,
If so, please buy me, we would have such fun,
A dog is just not for Christmas a dog is for life,
So if you are buying a dog, for my sake,
Please think twice.

*S. Parker*

# Too Late

She cares for pets, a foolish task
Why should she? Many people ask
After all, when all is said and done
They are only furry, hairy, toys, for fun.

I give mine food (most every day)
And when I'm bored they'll always play
The don't know the world in which we live
They take our time They cannot give.

I'm a caring owner, and always heed
My furry friends, (when they suit My need)
And if the owner's needs should cease
How convenient if the pets decease
A useful life and a tidy end
(It's not as if I've lost a friend).

You'd think shared years of man and beast
Would have taught me something, (to say the least)
Those dross emotions I've been spared?
Should I have loved? Should I have cared?

Could I learn to love, and realise
The message in those shining eyes
*"Our time's not scaled in days and years*
*It's built of love, and hopes and fears".*

*"The time we shared that you called "Living"*
*For me was spent in trust and giving*
*And as each day with you unfurled*
*You were the centre of my world"*

The writing's clear, for me to see
My pets were not just here for me
A life not filled with stale regrets
If I'd really learned to love my pets.

She cares for pets, a foolish task?
No, not so, since you care to ask
She pays our debts.  The ones we owe
As up above, so down below.

A small heaven from our earthly dust
For the friends who share her special Trust
So, help to make her living great
Don't be like me .....Don't be    **Too Late**.

To A.J. and all at Cinnamon

*Ron H.*

# My Very Own

I've just been sitting here thinking
How lucky can I get
To have such a lovely doggie
For my very own personal pet.

Your liquid eyes are pools of love
So trusting and sincere
And although you can't understand these words
I'm so very pleased your here.

The love you give is unlimited
You really are a treasure
To have you for my very own pet
Really is a pleasure.

So now I've told you how I feel
Even put it down in verse!
It's such a pity that you can't read -
(You would probably laugh - or worse!).

*Marion M. Hancock*

# The Attack

Cautiously scampering,
scraping for scraps
Frightenedly wondering,
Maybe, perhaps.

Will I get to try, a nibble of cheese,
A small drop of water,
I'm down on my knees.

Then all of a sudden,
A strong tasty smell
A whiff of pure excellence,
But then rings the bell.

Silently still,
Ears pricked and then
a 4-legged creature,
Softly wanders in.

Big teeth
      Sharp claws
      Round eyes
      - a pause.
Then ...... "Squeak!  Aah I'm dead!"
I'm flat on all 4's

*Amanda Marsh (Aged 12)*

# Hunter's Return or "Pain in the Rain"

With *"wellies"* on, thro' mud and rain,
into the woods I go again.
Its wet, its cold, can I be sane?
and now its dark, all down the lane.

Who cares about the armchair and the fire?
Its the outdoor life that I desire.
His head down, his tail is higher,
he's seen a rabbit, in the mire.

Then off he goes, leaving me dejected,
just when I need to be protected.
My faithful hound has just defected.

So then I wander home alone.
He's gone this time, I will never own a dog again,
perhaps a cat?

Oh! Who's that sitting on the mat?

### *Frank Mustill*

## Patch

His brown eyes would look at me
  His black and white tail
Would wag with glee
  I ask are we going for a walk
And he would bark as if he could talk
  He looked after me in his kind of way
Guarding me by night and day
  Many happy hours I did spend
Walking with my best friend
  Now I walk alone each day
Because my dog has passed away.

*Gwendoline Davies*

# Benji

Dark eyes look into mine.
A happy gaze says "Look at me",
see me jump and run about
then take me with you please.....

That is how our friendship started.
Now we're together, not often parted.

You travelled home upon my lap,
we'd not gone far when you had a nap.

To meet new friends.
To see new faces.
No walks at first in big open spaces.
No jabs were given in the other places.

You walked on two legs, not on four.
You pulled and tugged, you wanted more.

To training now we both do go.
Obedience, agility, you never will say no.

You sit and stay, you come to my call.
You play with the cats and you'll fetch a ball.

At times you're silly and act a clown.
You chase round the garden before you'll lay down.

You've grown into a lovely dog.
You've turned into a family friend.

It's made me often wonder why
the other people didn't try.

*Patricia Wells*

# Nervous

Here I am in my new bed

Nervous:

Looking round at my new home

Nervous:

Wondering what it will be like sleeping my first night

Nervous:

Wondering what they'll be like

Nervous:

After a day I felt a bit better

But I'm still

Nervous.

*Natalie Wells (Aged 8)*

# Sam

We wanted a pet dog
 A companion and a friend
Looking for one was very hard
It drove us round the bend
A healthy dog to care for
To give plenty T.L.C.
Crossbreed or mongrel or even pedigree
A visit to the rescue centre
Where I started to cry
A little dog sitting in the corner
We couldn't say goodbye
We've trained you well
You're new life has started
There's nothing wrong with you
You're so soft hearted
We take you for long walks
Which you thoroughly enjoy
Chasing footballs
Your favourite toy.
You cry at night which has become a habit
You must be dreaming of chasing a rabbit
In the past we don't know what you faced
But what we do know is that you can't be replaced.

*Alison Dodds*

# Daisy Dog

When Daisy Dog met Mr. Frog outside the garden shed
Asked Mr. Frog of Daisy Dog;

    "What was it that you said?"

Said Daisy Dog to Mr. Frog;

    "I only said 'Bow Wow'
    You can tell by that I'm not a cat
    Or else you'd hear me 'Meow'"

Daisy Dog's with Mr. Frog beside the garden pond.
It seems to me, it's plain to see, of him she's very fond.

I'm sure she sees him as a toy with which she likes to play,
He thinks, however, she's too rough and quickly hops away.

Daisy Dog, at first put out, soon finds another game,
Whilst Mr. Forg jumps in the pond, from which he'd shortly came.

Once safely in the pond again, he slowly raised his head
And watched as Daisy sniffed and searched a nearby flower bed.

She's clearly sniffed another friend, though who he
Couldn't see, his only thought of what she sought

    "I'm glad it isn't me."

*Donald Baker*

# Ode To Barney Joe

You were a furry, scruffy scrap
Who sat forlornly in my lap
Our very first dog
You were a comic from the start
Your funny yapping won my heart
You were fed and cuddled
You ate and puddled
Somehow we muddled through
We were both sad, when your master left
Puzzled and bereft
We walked and talked, played hide and seek
You licked the teardrops from my cheek
A good companion for fourteen years
Sunshine through the misty haze
Thank you for the happy days.

*Brenda Briar*

# Bingo

Round and round and turning
This way and that.
Grabbing at my ankles
Shaking the mat.
Stealing the dusters,
The dustpan and brush.
He's a mad little whirlwind,
A flash of white fluff.

In a moment of madness
In lunatic mood
Tissues get shredded
And furniture gets moved.
Slippers get shaken
His basket gets upturned
His drinking water paddled in
And me?  A bag of nerves.

He's a lively little Westie
But when he's asleep
He looks so calm and peaceful
And so innocent and sweet.
With his mouth slightly open
And his legs up in the air
He looks just like a fluffy toy
Sleeping in the chair.

He's absolutely barmy
But I'd never want him changed.
He's a pack of white naughtiness.
    Bingo is his name.

*Jennie Plane*

# The A to Z of Dogs

A is for Afghan, such an elegant hound, with long silky hair and a flowing bound.

B is for Bulldog, an English pride, proud and muscular, with an ambling stride.

C is for Cairn, a Terrier of sorts, bright button eyes, with a tail short.

D is for Dalmatian with it's many spots, well defined with plenty of dots.

E is for Elkhound, a strong wilful breed, whose ancestors date back to 4000 BC,.

F is for Foxhound whose staminas great, a tri-coloured coat and legs quite straight.

G is for German Shepherd, a worker he is, with a fine handsome head full of strong teeth.

H is for Hanover, so trustworthy and calm, an ideal breed as a gamekeepers alarm.

I is for Irish Setter, with plenty of zest, a coat of rich chestnut outstands the rest.

J is for Jack Russel, a lively, small chap, who chases rabbits and loves to yap.

K is for Komonodor, with a coat of white cords, strong and agile with a body quite broad.

L is for Labrador, the common family pet, in black, brown or yellow - they love getting wet.

M is for Mastiff of which there are few, Neopolitan and English are only just two.

N is for Norfolk who has no fears, a cheeky Terrier with V-shaped ears.

O is for Old English, a sheepdog you know, large and bold with much hair to show.

P is for Pit Bull, a breed wrongly condemned, so loyal and faithful on whom one can depend.

Q is for Quail Dog, a gun dog and swimmer, alas German Spaniel a right sporting winner.

R is for Rottweiler, intelligent and strong, a favourite of mine who can do no wrong.

S is for Scottie, squat, short and dandy, with a cute little beard and stern tail so handy.

T is for Tosa, the almighty of all, unfortunately banned for no reason at all.

U is for Ulmer Dogge or else the Great Dane, it's spectacular size has given it's name.

V is for Volpino Italiano, a mouthful of words, or Italian Spitz as it's more commonly heard.

W is for Whippet a racehorse of Hounds, graceful in spirit, body and bounds.

X is for Xoloitzcuintli, speak that if you can, Mexican hairless to you and all other man.

Y is for Yorkie so petitely designed. Whose coat is so soft, silky and fine.

Z is for Zande or Africa's Basenji, loyal and willing if ever was any.

This A to Z of dogs for you, are just to name all but a few,
So many to name, so many to choose, the list is endless, so its up to you.

*Mary Czornenkyj*

# "Help"!

Big dogs, fat dogs, eating lots of meat,
Small dogs, skinny dogs, needing more to eat,
Cute little puppies, left all alone,
Please, someone give them a home,
Left in a box,
Dinner for a fox
Dumped in the street,
That's not neat,
Some dogs sad, some dogs yappy,
Why can't we make all dogs happy!!

## Ceri-ann Busbridge King (Aged 13)

# Boosters!

How can my Wolfhound Ceilidh
Whose behaviour I praise daily
Each year contrive to fail me
On our visit to the vets?

Once inside, she senses dangers.
I assure the assembled strangers
As she quakes and whines
"She changes once she gets used to the vets".

One portly client teases
As he strokes his Bichon Frises
And his snooty pekineses
"She'll have you over, yet!".

Right on cue, she panics madly,
She pulls me, yanks me, snags me,
And behind his chair she drags me
As we wait to see the vet!

Now the centre of attention,
I attempt some intervention
Whilst the portly man howls loudly
And the receptionist gets upset.

The vet calms the Bichon Frises
And the snooty pekineses
But is forced down on his knees
As he jabs my unwilling pet.

So - the waiting room's upended,
With staff and clients offended,
But for a year my task is ended
My Wolfhound's <u>seen</u> the vet!

*Lyn Shawcroft*

# Christmas Joy

Christmas came with such joy,
Time to collect our Darling Boy,
Off we went to Leicestershire,
Full of hope and a little fear.

We drove along, our thoughts were mixed,
Will we manage, or will we be in a fix,
It's been a long time since we had a young Lad,
Will he be good or will he be bad.

Seven puppies were playing there,
Cuddly balls of fluff and fur,
Only one we can take away,
I'd like to stay with them and play.

But choose we must, I'd love them all,
The thin, the fat, the short and the tall,
This one stood out from the rest,
Whose looks just said, I'm the best.

I picked him up, this furry bundle,
Just had to give him a great big cuddle,
He just lay there and took all the fuss,
I'm almost certain that he chose us.

We called him Barney, home we came,
And very soon he knew his name,
He settled down and trained us well,
If he could speak what tales he'd tell.

*P. Rowley*

# Nicky

Inch by inch, you crawled towards me
Hesitant, trembling, and so unsure,
when I reached down to touch you
you cowered, and shook all the more.

It seems you were far too gentle
for a breed that should 'stand and fight'
so, you were kept tied up and beaten
for two years, this was your plight!

It broke my heart, as I realised
all you had ever known, was fear
No love, no fun, no happiness
just fright, when ever man came near!

I knew I could not leave you there
and so, I took you home with me
I was sure you'd be hard work
but, I won your trust eventually!

It took so long for you to learn
that you needn't cower in fear
and gradually, you gained confidence
when you knew that I was near.

You would rest your head on my knee
and sleep as though you hadn't a care
yet, every now and again look up at me
just to know, I was still there.

For ten years we were best friends
we formed a love and trust to share
where you were always by my side
my darling, faithful 'Teddybear'.

*Audrey Philps*

# Puppy's New Home

So small and warm, eyes of an angel
The puppy tanned with a band of
Black around it's nose
It leaps and trots through it's
New discovered wonderland.

Leafs dance and swirl in the autumn breeze
It chases round and round.
Pouncing, pawing, growling and barking
Before, turning to run into the house
And greedily lap up water.

Beautiful with fur so soft
It's next stop, is to visit it's bed
Softly, it's angelic black eyes
Close.  It sleeps away it's trials of today.

*S. Lacey*

# Dad's Birthday Ode

My doggy prayer was answered
When I found a Dad like you
I know that I'm not always good
But I'm faithful and I'm true
And so I wish you all the best
On this your special day
With all the love that's in my heart
More than woofs and barks can say.

*Palasco Jack*

## S. W. Fretwell

# The Strange Prayer

Oh God you made my life so colourless,
Just grey, black and white.
You made my tongue, all limp
And wet, no words I can recite.
I am but a humble stray Oh Lord
My coat is thick with mud,
My paws are hot and stinging
They leave a trail of blood.
I wish I could speak of my hopes and fears.
And Oh God!  When you made my eyes,
You forgot to give them tears.

*M. Weston*

# Susie

Susie was a pretty girl
Tall and black and stately,
Her thick coat had a handsome curl
Her temperament was saintly.

That is until she found a mate
Small and tan, called Scruff,
Who howled his heart out by the gate
And acted really tough.

Susie's now a happy madam
Scruff is acting sainted,
Conversant with the ways of Adam
The two are now acquainted.

### *Doreen Cartlidge*

# Two Spoiled Chihuahua's

There once was a puppy called Harry
and he was as happy as Larry.
But he couldn't talk
and nor would he walk.
He'd bang on your legs for a carry.

There once was a puppy named Rose
and for photos she just would not pose.
But if given a treat, she'd sit up real sweet
with chocolate all over her nose.

*R. T. Pearce*

# Pippa

Our Spaniel likes to roam all day
She loves to run and jump and play
She sniffs around for all new smells
What's under the hedges - she never tells
On walks in the field she meets all her friends
And when called to come home she always pretends
Not to hear! - But then she'll return,
Lessons of obedience she's beginning to learn.

Her favourite days are sunny and warm
Chewing a bone on a freshly cut lawn
Chasing squirrels and watching the rabbit
Teasing the birds, - as is her habit
She does lots of barking and making a noise
But then calms down and goes back to her toys.

In the afternoon it's time for her meal -
Now she knows how to follow to heel!
Finally at night she's glad of her bed
Somewhere safe to rest her dear head.

*Jenny Howard*

# A Cry In The Dark

Darkness comes over me, my life almost ended, no more playing or
being kindly tended.
No more rain or warmth from the sun, no more dreams or thoughts of
the run,
I lie in the gutter as people pass by, I'm shouting "I'm here and I'm still
alive".
Wind rustles the leaves, sends a chill through my fur, a passing voice
murmurs "Look at that cur".
Now where are my puppies taken cruelly away, they were only just born
when I heard someone say "Just kill them, they're trouble", but how can
that be,
I'd have nursed them and fed them if they'd left them with me.
Not so long ago I was loved and adored, food every day, toys littered the
floor.
The child who had loved me had got bored with it all, first I was moved
to a box in the hall.
Then came the time they said I must go, I wanted to shout "I still love
you" but no, I was shoved in a box and driven away, it seemed a long
time then I heard someone say,
"This is far enough, just throw her out here, there's no going back"
I shuddered with fear.
A lorry came rumbling at speed down the street, it hit me head on, I was
knocked off my feet -
With blood all around me I'm in terrible pain,
it soaks into my skin but's diluted by rain.
My eye's clouding over, I can't move my feet, my heart seems as though
it keeps missing a beat.  I'll just have to lie here, it won't be for long,
I'll lie here and wonder just what I did WRONG.

*J. Sherry*

# Come On In

Come on in little one
Do not look so sad,
Has your experience of man
Been so very bad?

Come on in little one
Your shaking will soon cease,
And you will learn to trust again
Your mind will be at peace.

Come on in little one
And meet the other crew
I know you won't believe it
But they were once like you.

They too have learned the hardest way
That man may not be 'friend',
They've born the brunt of kicks and blows
And longed for life to end.

But warmth, and care, and lots of love
Has turned their lives around.
They now believe in miracles
As changed lives they have found.

So, come on in little one
There's lots of things in store.
All of the things a dog likes best
And you will shake no more.

But, more than this my little one,
I know that I will see
Far more that I will give to you
Will be given back to me.

*Diana Gibb*

# Our Pals

Our first was Saddy, a mixture bitch,
On thundery night someone did ditch.
No injections, so distemper set in,
Them not looking after her was a sin.
Second, Lorry guard dog cross Alsation.
Prince, 2, cowed, thief, owner would abandon,
Husband brought him to me for love and care.
From day one no stealing, trust was there.
He was our friend, guardian, many long years,
At the age of twelve, he's gone we're in tears.
Elsa cross pointer was our third hill,
Got from a girl who's mother was ill
On pills, arthritus, a thief of school milk,
Police said keep home, her coat was like silk,
We took Kimbru Prince our poodle white.
To help Elsa's pain, give a good night,
Then six years later, he was on his own.
He quickly adapts to being alone.
X-rays to be taken, a cough has come,
His lungs full of tumours, we are struck dumb.
At work our son dies, in Scrubs London,
His Rottwieler Rommel, oh! What fun.
From London to Cardiff in a big van
We bring him to love, we know we can,
Within three years, his heart like our sons.
Goes bad, gives out, we miss him tons.
Nine months later got a bitch from the pound,
Part Wippet, Collie and some other hound,
Quick, clever year old, through the house she runs
White hazel chocolate, she's our options.

*Nicolette A. Thomas*

# Sandy

Sands you have a heart of gold,
but your thoughts cannot be told.

Your eyes are fierce, your teeth are strong,
but to me I know they will do no wrong.

Your golden coat shines in the light,
and by my bed you'll stay at night.

You are so faithful all the time,
it makes me glad that you're all mine.

A kiss from you each day my love,
means more to me than a golden dove.

Sandy how I love you so,
I never want to see you go.

*J. E. Hobbs*

# Kim

I remember one Sunday, when I was just four,
When my dad brought a bag of fun, through our front door.
He was soft, black and sable, a young German Shepherd,
Though in six months he took-on the size of a leopard.

He was no good for showing, for his tail wasn't right,
Though I grew to regard it, a quite normal sight.
And at four years of age, all that mattered it seems,
Was to watch his great leaps, over rivers and streams.

When I grew to my teens, he'd become my best mate,
And would wait every night, by our small garden gate.
Till at last, as I rounded the bend in the road,
I would call out his name and his mind would explode.

He'd hurry to greet me, with vigorous wagging,
Then leap to my shoulders, till my legs began sagging.
This ritual lasted till Mother appeared,
Then with tail twixt his legs, through the gate he'd be steered.

When you grow up with dogs and their loving inside you,
You accept they will always be right there beside you,
Yet Kim became ill, when I was just twenty,
The vet gave him treatment and loving a-plenty.

Then that cruel fateful day, as I turned twenty-one,
The vet told us Kim, just couldn't go on.
He was suffering great pain and it just wasn't fair,
To see the brave lad, just lie suffering there.

My pal passed away, in his home with his friend,
For a dog of his nature, a dignified end.
And I thought back to when this long friendship began.
I had laughed as a boy, now I wept as a man.
Now, twenty years later, my memories remain,
Of my faithful old Shepherd, with near-human brain.

**Mike Dawson**

# Pawmarks

Pawmarks in the kitchen, pawmarks in the hall,
Pawmarks on the doormat and even up the wall,
Muddy, dirty pawmarks are leading up the stairs,
Don't sit down before you look, the puppy loves the chairs!

We're trying to teach him - he doesn't have a clue,
Housetraining has become a game, but just who's training who?
He sniffs around in circles, so we grab him quick and run
But before we reach the garden, the little devil's "done".

He tells us that he's starving, he can't last out much more,
Perhaps the clocks have stopped, he's never been so starved before.
Quick, quick Mum, where's the chicken? It was due an hour ago,
What - milk again?? Oh no! A man needs substance don't you know?

He's a growling threatening mastiff, jaws slavering he's so cross.
That squeaky toy was ckeeky - better show it who's the boss.
He's fought and won another war, he's made another puddle,
Now it's time this little warrior curled up and had a cuddle.

He's really just a baby, tired out with all the fuss,
Thinks humans are a funny lot, they tell him off and cuss
But when he's curled asleep, before a new day's troubles start
He'll leave those little pawmarks printed over all your heart..

*A. S. Belsham*

# Born

I have but waited a lifetime for you to be born.
I planned you birth, even before your mother, was out of puppyhood.

I saw you born all wet, gasping for the cold night
air to fill your lungs.

I looked at your soft fur shiny satin, the colour of fire,
hot glowing red.  Muzzle of black as deep black coal.

Your eyes not yet open, but I closed my eyes.
I could see in my imagination, that your eyes
will be shiny clear and radiant brown.

That day is long gone, years have gone by!
the fun and delight in our company together, is
past as in a quickening of an eye.

The light and soul has faded eventide came a calling!
I did take your head in my arms and stroked your
noble head, then kissed you the long goodbye.
Your eyes faded as life's true spirit left you!

This cold wet night another is born, full of magic
with fire of life!
I see you in her, my faithful friend.
I see her deep black muzzle, her fur as soft
satin, the colour of red hot fire.

*Helen Pearson*

## Rhanna's Dinner

Our little Rhanna she is so keen
She'll eat almost anything that she has seen
Bacon and mutton or beef or ham
I've even seen her try bread and jam.

but her favourite I think is the food that she pinches
To the other dog's plates she creeps up by inches
She opens her mouth and dives in and then
Before they can stop her she's gone again.

She crams the food in like a hamster she looks
They didn't write this in the Sheltie Yearbooks
Then off to a corner to eat at her leisure
I think it's the stealing that gives her such pleasure.

*David C. Irwin*

# The Four Seasons Of Love

SPRING
>Is their puppyhood
Where they are taught whats bad, and whats good,
And what in life is to be done
All their knowledge learnt in games of fun.

SUMMER
>They are so full of play
With heaps of energy throughout the day.
It's 5.o'clock and mine's out of his bed
He's by the bowl, waiting to be fed.
O' Rover it's cold outside, it's starting to hail
I suppose I have to take you for that walk
Waggle the tail.

AUTUMN
>They are supposedly mellow
But no-one told the rules to my loving fellow
For he still loves to run, chase, jump and gambol
Up hill over dale in one big scramble.

WINTER
>I can now see snowflakes upon his face
He still enjoys his games but with more grace
He will never be old
Just a slower pup
Like J. M. Barry's creation
He will never, in my mind grow up.

*A. Jones*

# Ode of a Travelling Dog

I love my mistress
My mistress loves me
One day she'll send me
Across the sea

No more walks
No more runs
Just six months
Without any fun

No loving cuddles
No lovely meals
Just bowls of food
And monotony

I have my chip
I have had my jabs
I can give blood
For a passport, Ma'am

Better than being smuggled through
In a boot and drowsy too
Hiding like a criminal
Not proud and free - like I am

These human things
Don't realise
Six months quarantine
It's hell inside

All this doesn't need to be
MAFF
WAKE UP
A passports what I need.

*Hexe (Fuller)*

## *J. Fuller*

# With Nan On The Sands Of Dee

Across the shining shore towards the Island,
Under white scudding clouds she flies along,
Free as the larks that rise up from the sand dunes
To fill the sky with shrill exultant song.

This is the place to be; our private Eden,
Alone together between sky and earth,
Salt laden air, and green beyond the River
The sunlit hills of Wales that gave her birth.

I whistle, and a small speck in the distance
Turns and comes racing swiftly back to me;
Becomes a dog, a little Border Collie,
Rejoicing in her time of liberty.

With sea-wet fur and sand upon her muzzle,
And laughing eyes she glances up at me,
As we walk on, content with one another,
In Collie Heaven, on the Sands of Dee.

*P. Borrows*

# Barking

Out there training together
In all kinds of weather
Most people think that we're not very bright
And there are times, you know
In the rain, frost and snow
You'd have to agree that they're right.

But you've got to admit
That they do keep us fit
And slow down the approaching senility
At least that's *my* excuse
For why else would we choose
To devote half our lives to Agility?

*Carl Stretton*

# Our Lucy

Our Lucy's gone to heaven above,
On earth she was a dog to love.
Nothing on earth can take her place,
Not even from the human race.

Together we spent happy days,
and I soon got to know her ways.
Often when out for a walk,
she'd do most everything but talk.

Sadly we knew not from the start,
that Lucy had a failing heart.
We tried so hard but all in vain,
Nothing could put it right again.

And looking back on all the years,
ones eyes begin to fill with tears.
Recalling all those happy days,
Of Lucy's soft and gentle ways.

When friends called round she'd never fail,
to greet them with a wagging tail.
She'd never growl or try to bite,
in spite of other dogs that might.

To us she was the perfect friend,
and how we missed her at the end.
She's gone to those kennels in the sky,
But in our thoughts she'll never die.

Perhaps as years go flying by,
We'll visit those kennels in the sky.
And maybe on a heavenly plane,
we'll see our Lucy once again.

*J. K. Webster*

# Muffin - Our 'Little Girl'

She's white with spots on her tail and her ears
She acts like a puppy, belying her years,
One bundle of mischief with eyes full of fun,
So eager to greet us when days work is done.

Only pet owners will know what we mean,
Hair everywhere, house never clean,
These things don't matter to her 'Mum and Dad'
'Our little girl' could never be bad.

She has her choice of all the chairs,
We have to move when she stands and stares.
We love every whisker and each little curl.
She's MUFFIN, she's special, she's 'OUR LITTLE GIRL'.

*Sheila M. Gannon*

# Why Bark?

Well now, I'm a dog if you know what I mean -
Four legs, nose and tail with a bark in between.
The legs are for running, the tail's there to wag,
The nose is to sniff with, but the bark has a snag.

I regularly choose all the wrong times to bark -
When I'm answering the door or patrolling the park,
If I'm warning off thieves or repelling a foe,
Even wrong when I'm telling a cat where to go!

I can't bark at dogs, cats, mice, rabbits or voles,
Neither squirrels, stoats, weasels, geese, chickens or moles.
It seems that I'm wrong even opening my trap -
"Just shut up you cur or you'll get a good slap!".

Those two dogs down the road can just bark as they please,
There's a hole in their fence - I walk past just to tease.
The man they belong to stands shouting at me
So I just use his gatepost for having a pee.

Last night I struck lucky - I got my own back.
In the dark of the night a man with a sack
Came through our back window - from me? Not a peep!
I just closed my eyes and pretended to sleep.

In the morning a policeman came round to our house
"What's the use of a dog if he's quiet as a mouse?
The man down the road doesn't get his house burgled".
I laughed when my owners blushed, spluttered and gurgled.

*M. A. Stone*

# Charlie is a Staffy

Fat and round and wobbly,
"A boxer pup?" they'd say.
"No, Charlie is a Staffy",
I'd watch them edge away.
It's true you were no angel,
Those little teeth kept flashing;
Coffee table eaten,
Chairs and birdcage crashing.
Visitors tormented:  Hurtling at their knees,
Chomping on their shoes,
Hanging off their sleeves.
When you'd been well-scolded,
You'd roll a scornful eye,
And I would stand despairing
As you went strutting by.

Well, you've improved with age, and training,
Though the haughty look's still there,
And the saucy swagger,
And the 'Don't care' air.
But - So's that Staffy smile, and ever-wagging tail,
And the never-failing wicked charm
That I've come to know so well.
Yes, Charlie is a Staffy,
But she's so much more beside:
Gentleness and laughter,
Loyalty and pride.
So if you meet us walking,
Please don't turn to flee -
It's not some hairy monster,
It's only Chas - and me.

*S. Hemsley*

# For Poppy

My little yellow dog, today
did not raise a wagging tail
she lay upon the bed she loved
as her life began to fail
she looked to me with eyes of love
and raised her head in grief
I held her tightly in my arms
and we both began to weep.
My little yellow dog,
had reached her final breath,
we shared everything together,
in life, in fun, in death.

My Poppy dog has gone from here,
my house is not the same,
she had to got, I told her go,
but a part of her will always remain.
My little yellow dog is everywhere
- yet nowhere I can see
my little yellow Poppy dog
means all the world to me.

*Sue Hemmings*

# The Stray

Taken to a new home at eight weeks old,
I was a cute and fluffy pup.
There I lived with three children who loved me,
But then sadly, I grew up.

No longer was I like a cuddly toy.
The children cried, "We're bored with that."
"We don't want it anymore," they grumbled.
"We'd much rather have a cat."

Kicked out of the house with no-one to care,
All alone now, just left to roam.
Crossing main roads, feeding on scraps from bins.
Not wanted in my old home.

Winter arrived and snow covered the ground,
The damp, cold and dark nights grew long.
My once thick coat became brittle and sparse.
Whatever had I done wrong!

I tried to keep warm as best as I could,
Curled up under a bush or tree.
The wandering life was making me weak,
What was to become to me.

But then just in time my saviour came.
She picked me up and shook her head,
"You poor little thing," I could hear her say.
"To me you look almost dead."

Now warm and fed, I curl up at her feet,
She loves me and says I'm clever.
And she has made me a promise that I
Can stay with her forever.

**_G. Fountain_**

# Untitled

I know my mistress loves me, and trusts me to behave,
And when another dog appears I'm very, very brave.
I bark at window cleaners, and growl at strangers too,
And when an unknown voice is heard I know just what to do.
If I am on my own at home, I'd trouble any thieves -
So why is it, when Autumn comes, I'm terrified of <u>leaves</u>!

*E. Wagener*

# Heidi

20-7-79 to 27-1-95

I treated you with tenderness
And lots of loving care
Now my heart is broken
Because you're no longer there
Oh! Heidi how I loved you
Right from the very start
When as a tiny puppy
You crept into my heart
You were my loyal and loving friend
Happy and faithful right up to the end
I'd rub my face into your fur
And whisper sweet nothings in your ear
As the weeks and months roll by
I often think of you and cry
It was the worst day of my life
When I had to say goodbye
God bless my faithful Heidi
Until we meet again.

Your loving Mum

*Joan Gooch*

# Rescued

For there he sits all alone,
lost and lonely, just wanting a home.
People pass and take no notice,
and all because he seems quite boisterous.

As we pass from cage to cage,
he cached my eye, and I give a sigh.
A funny looking mutt indeed,
wanting attention, and his very own lead.

I ask whats happened to this dog,
for the reply, he's a handful and found in a sack.
At once I knew to rescue him,
that sad little face, and oh so thin.

For now he is lonely no more,
he's very happy and not so poor!
No more cages, no more peering eyes,
the cruelty that befalls are friends
but, for this lucky dog, his tale ends.

For Tizer, my rescue dog.

*Wendy Gould*

# Who Dug That Hole

*Told By Ben (Boots) Brown*

Who dug that hole I heard you say.
It wasn't there just yesterday.
You filled up all my other ones
And threw away my juicy bones.

Nicknamed Boots though it's a fact
Why people think I can be
As bossy as that black and white cat
Who sits on the fence and stares at me.

I'll dig a hole and then he'll see
Who's cleverer, him or me.
Of my barks, he takes no heed
Wait till I see him off my lead.

I have a lovely row of holes now.
Think I'll get the blame somehow.
Would you believe it was the moles
That peppered all the hedge with holes.

I'm just a little cavalier chap
With big brown eyes and wagging tail
Who gets forgiven each mishap
I know if all else fails:
I'll blame it on a herd of snails.

*Jean Brown*

# I Only Wanted To Love You

*(Cry of an abandoned dog)*

I only wanted to love you,
That's all I wanted to do.
I only wanted to love you
And be your best friend too.

You only had to feed me
And regularly take me out
And I'd protect you all my life,
Of that there is no doubt.

It didn't seem a lot to ask
That you should care for me,
When all my love and life were yours,
But it was not to be.

If you had only shown me
What you wanted me to do,
Perhaps it would have worked out then;
I really did love you!

But why did you abuse me
And turn me out to die,
Without a parting word or pat,
No explanation, why?

I only wanted to love you.

*T. Betty Chadwick*

# Spring-Heeled Jack

It is not long, the lifetime of a dog,
A span of fourteen years, or little more,
From when the puppy greets each day, agog,
Till, full of age, he scarce can lift a paw.
Sometimes on woodland walks, in dappled light,
Or in a leaf-lined, chalkland country dell,
I still can see a flash of brown and white,
A springer hot on some old squirrel smell.
Or, midst the rustling stalks of flax, long dead,
His busy body scurrying here and there,
Butterfly ears a-flap above his head,
Springing to scan the field, the trees, the air.
And still I hear him scamper on the floor
Impatient for the opening of a door.

He chased, and robbed from rooks their hard-earned crust,
Harried the pheasants vainly through the wood,
Rolled in the cowpats, relished foxes' must,
Feasted on things that only he thought good.
He used to hunt the mallards on the lake
Till they escaped him in the willow copse,
Then, close to me, he'd give a hearty shake,
Making a scattered rainbow of the drops.
At dusk, he'd flop upon his favourite seat,
Sleep through a twitching dream of hunt and chase,
Yet still alert to sounds of nearing feet,
Ready to jump and lick his master's face.
And I still hear the sharp, commanding bark,
"Come, let me in, I'm waiting in the dark!".

*S. Morris*

# Deacon

A super dog I know is Deacon,
A dog with eyes that shine like a beacon.
He likes nothing better than a run in the park
Especially when the night is dark.
To sniff out rabbits or a fox or two
He outruns his friends with little ado.

His coat is smooth like pussy willow,
But he likes his comfort, he has his own pillow!
A gentle dog, companion and friend
Faithful and proud to the very end.

So come on Deacon let's not delay
Its time to take you out to play.
To enjoy the sights and smells around
To gallop ahead, energy abound.
To outrun all is just a snippet
After-all you are a whippet!

**_Margaret Matheson_**

# Dog Trainer ... Where Are You?

Training classes are just too much for me,
All those breeds creating havoc, blimey!

Barking mad, that's what I am, I'm sure,
Watching for the next "Whoopsy" on the floor!

Hoping to be heard once in a short while,
So to demonstrate the sit, stay and smile!

But will I get a word in now, tonight?
Things are so loud, it will take a dog fight!

So, brains are now needed so to succeed,
Get the biscuits out, so all can now feed!

Then run like hell out from all of the class,
Hoping a dog won't chase you, and bite your...

Then after a break come back in and start,
And don't be put off again, by one bark!

Because your needed, and must give a toss,
Because your determined, and your boss!

*Debra Neale*

# Lucy

Little Lucy Locket
Born to be our love
We hope that you are happy
In heaven up above

We hope you get your biscuits
and walks everyday
We really miss you
now that you have gone away

The house is not the same now
All neat and tidy
But we preferred the hairs and crumbs
and you snoring loudly

Please wait for us to join you
As we surely will one day
And then we'll have such fun together
and play & play & play

We will cuddle like we used to
and never again say goodbye
Until then our love be happy
and we will try not to cry.

## E. Turnbull

# Merlyn

A tiny puppy in a box,
Travelled home from Wales,
So quiet and apprehensive,
As the car ate up the miles.

A glorious liver coat he grew,
So handsome, so debonair,
He sat with his back so very straight,
His nose up in the air.

He ran and jumped, enjoyed his life,
Chasing squirrels. cats and rabbits,
We could not stop him any way.
He got into very bad habits.

He put up with the children,
With Amber, Zak and Gem
He did not once snap or snarl,
Just sighed and turned away from them.

And then the light began to fade,
His eyes grew steadily dimmer,
His coat less shiny and not so dark,
He became a little thinner.

He passed away at Christmas,
To the kennel in the sky,
He'll run and jump and play there too,
Just like the times gone by.

*Lea Wright*

# My Dog At My Side

As I sit here.  With my dog at my side
She looks, up at me.  Her love.  She can't hide.
Her paw on my arm.  To let me know.
She'll always, be here.  And will never go.
When humans, forsake me.  My dog never will.
Whatever I do.  She loves me still.
When I tell her, my troubles.  She listens to me.
At my side.  My friend, will, always be.
Whatever the future has in store.
My dog, will be, beside me.  For evermore.

*Maureen Roberts*

# Ode to a Dragon

I know a friendly dragon
Tinkerbell's her name
And I have been so happy
Since into my life she came

She has no wings to speak of
On her short and wrinkly back
Her feet are small and catlike
With claws thick strong and black

Tinkerbell's not scaly
But this does not bother her
Instead she wears a good disguise
Of brown and bristly fur

She has no horns upon her head
Her brow furrowed and crinkly
But she does have tiny shell-like ears
And eyes deep brown and twinkly

She's not a magic dragon
So she cannot grant me wishes
Instead she wags her curly tail
And gives me hugs and kisses

She cannot breath out sparks of flame
So maybe I am wrong
No wait, just look inside her mouth
She has a purple tongue!

People stop and stare at us
As we go our merry way
Amused by lovely Tinkerbell
Dragon or Shar-Pei?

**Sharon Holland**

# From Their Point Of View

No such thing as a Sunday to laze round the house
If you'd wanted that we'd suggest a pet mouse
A lie in is something just un-heard
And holidays abroad are of course quite absurd.

A long walk, training and a good feed
Are really all we require and need
We're quite happy to try this thing called Agility too
But when you give the wrong signs what's a dog to do.

At times you shout if we do it wrong
It's not our fault you said "tunnel" not "long"
Some days we get up early to go to a show
We take the wrong course, how were we to know.

We also love Flyball, it's such great fun
Trying to break the record as fast as we can run
We get so excited on the start line
Oh do let us go now and we'll be fine.

And as for Obedience it's a little more relaxed
But at times our poor brains do get taxed
Left turns, heelwork, retrieves and a down stay
Oh sorry I didn't do a very good send away.

Sometimes you're not pleased we can easily tell
A dropped scent cloth or that pole that fell
All for nothing that long journey in the car
Never mind, who knows one day we may go far.

But best of all at the end of the day
We know you'll always love us come what may
And just remember we dogs are for life
Rather like a husband or a wife.

**Sue Culmer**

# Solace's New Hobby

Solace has a new hobby!
Collecting snails, one by one,
Some full shells and some are empty.
What is that, I've just stepped on?
Another snail has hit the dust!

Are they brought indoors as 'prezzies'?
No!  Just something else to play with.
When she is tired of playing with one,
She is off to find another.
Gretchen looks down, so dignified!
Harry says, "that's nice"...

At least I'm now up to her tricks (I hope)
and look carefully where I tread.

Solace!!!  What have you got in Gretchen's bed??
She looks up so pleased and loving, all innocent, of course,
It's alright Mum, it's only my snail...

What can you say, what can I do...
She is only young once.

## *P. M. King*

# My Dog

Such a pleasure,
To take on a walk.
Silent;
Unable to talk.

Knows not the evil of selfishness or pride,
Has no secrets to hide.
Is affectionate and friendly;
More trustworthy than any friend.
My best friend, he will remain,
Until his life's end.

But the sad point to this tale.
Is that, dogs do not live
As long as human-beings.
So, one day,
I will have to get another.
But no other can take his place.
He belongs to a superior race.
His obedience shows dignity and grace.

*Linda Webster*

# Forever

Adorable is the pup,
with a key to your heart
who's exuberance and zest,
is a joy from the start.

Comical is the youngster
he's an explosion of fun,
as he explores his new world,
his innocent life just begun.

Grateful is the dog
for rewards of love and play,
for walks in fields of daisies,
where time evaporates away.

Loving is the dog,
with his deep, soulful eyes,
intelligent and honest,
he will tell you no lies.

Loyal is the dog,
who licks away your tear,
who will rest while you sleep
content to be near.

Devoted is the dog,
he's the refreshing spring breeze,
he's the warmth of late summer sun,
and the beauty of autumn leaves.

Forever is a dog,
who's by your side until you part.
Then, forever, he will be,
the pup who won your heart.

*J. A. Naseby*

## Lines For A Staffordshire Bull-Terrier
## Resting On His Stomach

Patting, with confident affection,
A crack-shin skull of white-brushed black,
They talked about his predilection
For lying on his broad flat back,
Duly admired those jaws' huge muscles,
That short coat and its natural gloss,
And temper kept through romps and tussles -
*It's true, he's almost never cross.*

Alas, the supple pup that bounded,
Last night, as if he might take wing,
Is now, the morning after, grounded,
A watch-dog with a weakened spring
Who cannot rise to greet his master,
Just yet, without a certain risk
Of still worse vertebral disaster -
*He's, roughly speaking, slipped a disc.*

Spine uppermost to anxious bendings,
His plight reminds how years abridge
Dogs' days with inelastic endings,
Their capers like their cartilage -
Though hints of such a stiffer finish
Long stay beyond a patient's ken
Whose vet swears, as the pangs diminish,
*He'll soon be on his back again!*

### G. E. Rome

# Fidelity

Please don't despair when I'm no-longer near,
Life is too short to bear sorrow.
Recall times we shared, and try not to fear
The emptiness of tomorrow.

My pretty brown eyes, once so bright, now are old.
My golden hair's sprinkled with grey.
The sun's lost its heat, and the winter's so cold -
I am ready, release me I pray.

I shall rest peacefully knowing I've been
Your guardian, your servant, your friend.
And I know that one day, yet to come, unforeseen,
Our cruel separation will end.

For remember, however long you may be,
As always, I'll patiently wait.
With my toy and a wagging tail, there I'll be
To greet you - at Heaven's gate.

*Julia Wrathall*

# Nikita

She's standing proud, alone, untamed
Siberian Husky she's been named
Her soul is filled with the call of the wild
Yet her manner is gentle, loving, mild.

Darkest eyes hide mysteries deep
Ancestral secrets forever to keep
She doesn't need to bark or howl!
Those eyes express all, fair or foul!

This dignified little lady's my friend
To her needs and wants I happily attend
Sometimes aloof, demanding respect
She will be my companion, but never my pet.

At her happiest killing Seaweed on the shore
Playing in the snow, or if by the fire she can snore
Yet hers is a spirit that will not be broken!
Especially when the ancestral hunter's awoken.

Exuberant with a joy for living
A nature that's loyal and very forgiving
She'll do as she is bid - if she must
It's such an honour to have her trust.

So glad I chose that dreamy, fluffball of a puppy
With her to share my life, I count myself lucky!
She should be running wild and free!!
But I hope she's happy to stay with me.

*Laurna McKie*

# The Waiting Game

This was a new game!
She wagged her tail
As she stood by the road, ready,
Frail legs stiff in the early morning air.

To her nostrils, smells seemed strange,
Not the familiar scents of home,
Nor her usual walk round the block,
(If she was lucky).

She had leaped so joyfully into the boot!
Car meant park, games, fun, no lead.
She waited patiently for a command.
Was this a new game?

They hadn't said 'Stay!' - just driven away.
So what WAS the game?
She would lie down and wait,
And wait and wait and wait ....

*Phillipa Ferst*

## "Caninekind"

**By Amos the Mongrel (written when he was 2 years old)**

O why do people speak of "humankind"?
If it was always true I would not mind.
But some of them are not so kind at all,
especially to dumb creatures, weak and small.

This woman stands at edge of field with stick
to whack her dog, on lead - she must be thick !
He hangs his tail for fear of being beaten;
thinks "exercise" means passing what he's eaten.
He longs to run about and play with me
and all my friends, but on his lead stays he.

Mum tells me "Leave that dog", although she knows
he longs to run with me and stretch his toes.
But I feel sorry for him.  He should know
that <u>someone</u> loves him; so to him I go.
She raises her big stick at me - what fun!
I jump and snatch the stick.  Away I run
and take it straight to Mum, who hands it back
and tells the woman, "If I see you smack
your dog or any other with this stick
the RSPCA will find out quick".

Change "humankind" to "those folk all mixed up".
Let "caninekind" mean each dog, bitch and pup.

*Deborah M. Berry*

125

# The Dog Alphabet

A is for all dogs, be they terrier or hound,
B is for bathtime, suddenly he's nowhere to be found.
C is for chasing, whatever gets in his way,
D is for din-dins, the best part of the day.
E is for exercise, one of his basic needs,
F is for flowers, he digs up roses not weeds!
G is for grooming, he may need brushing each day,
H is for heart, he'll steal yours away.
I is for intelligence, he learns quick and is eager to please,
J is for jumping, on a pair of inviting knees.
K is for kennel, the outdoor home for the tough,
L is for love, your dog can't have enough.
M is for money, he'll use up plenty of yours,
N is for naughty, chewed furniture, muddy paws.
O is for old age, when he needs extra care,
P is for poorly, a time he'll want you there.
Q is for quarrelsome, with some dogs he'll fight,
R is for rolling, cow pats are a special delight!
S is for sympathy, he knows just how to win ours,
T is for toys, he'll squeak his favourite for hours.
U is for understanding, sensitive to each other's mood,
V is for vets, when he isn't feeling too good.
W is for walkies, out in all kinds of weather,
X is for kisses, he's your friend forever.
Y is for youthful, he'll keep you that way,
Z is for ZZZzzzz., peace, at the end of his day.

*Lynne Hanson*

# Our Dog Called Sheba!

There was a dog called Sheba,
who had lots of toys,
she'd bite 'em and squeak 'em and
pull 'em and eat them
and make lots of noise.

She likes to run on the common,
and pull on branches of trees,
then she would scrape lots of big
holes, then squat for her wee-wee's.

She would spend about an hour,
running and jumping about,
but that's our little baby,
      Madam Sheba Mount.

*Gina Downing*

# Ode To Ben

He is gone, my Ben, yet ever near
I saw his eyes dim, once so clear,
''twas only yesterday, they opened to greet the world
A fluffy bundle, in a basket curled.
I'm thankful for the hours we shared,
The fun, the work, knowing he cared,
For the paw that rested in my hand
The look that said I understand.
He gave his all, and now, alas he's gone
But not quite, you see, I have his lovely Son.

*Iris M. Newbould*

# Tips For A Debuting Dog-Exhibitor (For Medve)

Well you're ready to go
And you must know we're so concerned your first show is a pleasure
So we send this advice
(and include in the price) a poem thrown in for good measure.

The day before showing
Be sure you are knowing your tank's full, and you've packed your pass
or you'll get to the gate
In a hell of a state, 'cause they won't let you into your class.

Now, keeping your head
It's early to bed before rising to shine on the day
A minimal breakfast
Ensures that the trek just goes smoothly - no "stops" on the way !

You go into your class
See the others at last, and pray you compare with the rest
You eye them, they eye you,
(You could do with the loo) but remember you're showing the best.

Toes and fingers are crossed
But all will not be lost, if the first time its not victory,
There's no cause for sorrow
There's always tomorrow, and next time a judge who can see.

When your dog's looking handsome
To meet with a man somewhat lacking good judgement is hard
But stand, grin and bear it
At home you can swear, hit the bottle and rip up your card.

If a win comes your way
Make the most of your day, success is both fickle and fleeting,
Keep your feet on the ground
Because next time around, you could take a hell of a beating !

*Jan McLeod*

# In Memory Of Kym

I wonder if you hear me call, speak your name, and cry?
Oh how I miss that little face, body warm and wonder why - why - why?
He needed you, but must have known, just how much love from my life
                                                            was torn.

I love you Kym, oh the pain as I call your name - you never came,
I held you tight - you seemed to know that God had called - to him you
                                                            had to go,
If only I could have died and <u>we</u> had gone - oh dear God, what did I do
                                                            so wrong?

To make you take the one I loved so very much,
The love of my life and a joy to touch,
Kym gave so much, never questioned why, why dear Lord?  Why did he
                                                            die?

How can I go through this again, with two more dogs who mean so
                                                            much?
Full of life and wonderful to love.
We have so much fun and laughter, high jinks, happiness, sometimes
                                                            disaster,
But always the love and companionship that mean so much ----

Kym's little body is missing, my hand to touch and cuddle, what a life,
What a muddle,
Please, please, when I die, with all my dogs let me lie,
Free to walk and roam - with my little Kym - and all my dogs - at home.

## *Pat Westhead*

# Holly's Day

I'm really very tired today,
Mum keeps throwing the ball away
I've chased the cat into his tree
That'll teach him to sit there, spitting at me!
I've dug the lawn and weeded the beds.
Don't pansies look better without their heads?
We've been to the park
For some workout and play,
Lots of 'sits' and 'downs'
A 'fetch' and a 'stay'.
Then home for a nap with my head on Mum's lap.
Dinner smells lovely, but what's this I've got?
Not roast beef or turkey, not steak or hot pot,
But boring old kibble, I'll throw up the lot!
Now that it's dark, it's leash for me,
'Cos out in the garden Mum cannot see.
One last little game, oh not that again!
Why oh why, when I want to play
Does Mum always start throwing the ball away?

*Barbara Ann Hamlyn*

# Rescued

His brown eyes stared beseechingly into mine
Challenging me not to turn away.
I'd walked past him by then,
And turned to see him lean sadly on the bars of his prison.
Something undefinable drew me back.
He was sad, lonely, devoid of human contact.
"I'll have him" - the lady smiled and took my money.

Three days later I brought him home.
Without prison bars to bind him, his character changed.
We went everywhere together -
Two lonely souls finding solace in each other.
Mischief glinted in his once sad eyes -
A guilty face peeped from behind every corner.
I hadn't the heart to tell him off -
His loyalty and devotion have repaid me many times over.
A truer friend I have never found, than in Jasper,
My 'adopted' dog.

*Ruth Brideoake*

# A Tale Of Two Terriers

Come on you strange human fellows
Get your heads up off those pillows
Now you stir as we lick your faces
Oh how strange the human race is!

Everyday you wash and dress
You look so funny we must confess
But still we will not be complaining
We're off for our walk, and if it's raining
There's a choice of coats, and then it's training
Interspersed with lots of play
At various intervals throughout the day.

Each afternoon we're brushed and combed
And walked again until Dad's phoned
We'll have our tea and pick him up
And tell him what us lucky pups
Have done today and who we've met
And tell him we're not finished yet
Still time to play with squeaky toys
And bones and make lots of noise.

Then suddenly it's getting late
Our baskets are calling there's no mistake
Take us up to bed please Dad
What a busy day we've had
We'll dream about tomorrow's dog class
And keep our warm brown eyes closed fast
Goodnight to our Mum and Dad
We're the best dogs that they've ever had.

*K. P. Thornby*

# The Annual Basset Hound Picnic

At Glenbrook Park in July of each year,
Basset Hounds gather from far and near;
one by one and in pairs they appear
    at the annual Basset Hound picnic.

Hounds of every size and colour
seem genuinely glad to see one another;
some even greet a sister or brother
    at the annual Basset Hound picnic.

There's Noodles, Cruiser, Patti, and Maggie,
Alex, and Dolly with the tail so waggy.
All of their suits are a little too baggy
    at the annual Basset Hound picnic.

Not one dog ever utters a growl,
but cover your ears when they start to howl.
Streams of slobber drip from each jowl
    at the annual Basset Hound picnic.

After they finish lunch there's a race;
the contestants course at a staggering pace
with ears a-flap and a smile on each face
    at the annual Bassett Hound picnic.

For the winner, victory's always sweet;
the prize is a box of his favourite treat.
The fact that *any* dog wins is a feat
    at the annual Bassett Hound picnic.

After the howl-off and race, they all nap
on a comfy blanket or someone's soft lap;
drifting to dreamland is always a snap
        at the annual Bassett Hound picnic.
When finally it's time to say adieu
one by one, or two by two
everyone says, "We'll be seeing you
        at the annual Bassett Hound picnic.

*Sue Wright*

# My Friend

I call your name,
You bound to heel,
I talk, we walk,
You sit, I kneel,
A friendly hug,
A stroke, a pat,
A paw to hold,
A tail to wag.

Someone to listen,
A presence to feel,
Something to cling too,
Someone who's real,
No hidden agenda,
No pain to impart,
Just total acceptance,
At one with my heart.
Eyes full of innocence,
Trusting and free,
A spirit unfettered,
Bounding to me.

*Trevor Warner*

# Bruno's Tale

For twelve long months I sat there waiting for you to arrive;
I greeted every visitor, and for affection I did strive.
You found me in a corner of a small and dingy shed;
I fought for food with others, and had papers for my bed.

I knew when I first saw you, that you would bring me cheer;
A happy home to live in and a family to be near.
It took me one whole hour to realise sofas were just fine;
And fires were warm to sit by, and a dish put down was mine.

For twelve long months I waited for someone to call my own;
Now I have love and laughter where once I felt alone.
I didn't know where I came from, I was too young to know;
But I am so glad you chose me, and I'll always love you so.

You say I make you happy, keep you fit and on your mark;
I tell you when the postman comes - for then I always bark.
I frank the mail a second time, just to check it's not alive;
And always take the paper in if I hear the boy arrive.

For twelve long months I lay there in that cold and draughty shed;
But now I have thick blankets, and a special comfy bed.
I dream sometimes of those dark days and always hope and pray
That each and every dog in there finds happiness one day.

*Wendy J. Wearing*

# Eternal TLC

The village did not miss him for a while.
All knew he had not kept a dog of late.
A straight and honest man, and with no guile:
He would not leave a dog to random fate.
Throughout his life the dogs were many, that he had taken in;
And he'd never stint a penny on their care through thick and thin.
Some came to him with pleading eyes.
Some beseeched with upraised paw.
He accepted all with no surprise;
And all were safe once at his door.

Long known about the village, with a swirl of dogs about his coat,
An old felt hat, brown cords and boots, a knitted muffler at his throat.
He was known to have an income: It went out as it came in;
And supported, in his cottage, dogs of unknown kith and kin.
And sometimes he would travel, if ever word there came,
To save a dog abandoned, ill treated, sick or lame.
If someone scorned his way of life, he would placidly reply:
It is you who are the loser: There's more to dogs than meets the eye.
Some would scornfully suggest, how very lonely he must be.
He would simply smile and answer: No, my dogs are here with me.

They found him taken to his bed.
Among a ghostly canine pack he lay.
The cottage humble as a shed;
The old man passive, as chilled as clay.
They heard him speak to the restless throng:
Come on now - stop this din -
Just wait a while - I won't be long -
Then we shall all go in -
And on his stone is stated simply, plain there for all to see:
My happiness is eternal, for my dogs are here with me.

*Patrick Lane*

139

# Who's Always There

Who made those mucky paw prints
That spread across the floor
Who's made my armchair hairy
And scratched the paint off the front door.

Now who's bit the postman
And chewed up the Royal mail
Who knocked the Royal Dolton
Off the table with his tail.

But who's always there to greet me
When I come in from the rain
Who licks away my tears
And makes me smile again.

Who snuggles up beside me
When I go to bed at night
To chase away the nightmares
And make everything alright.

*Mandie Hart*

# A Little Boy's Wish

"Can we have a dog"
Said the little boy.
"Remember" said his mum
"A dog is not a toy,
They have feelings
The same as you and me
They love to hear you talk
And go for daily walks
Round about the trees
You, have to give it a name
So that it will come
       when you call
They just love playing with a ball
       love it the same
As I love you
And we will see
       What we can do".

## *D. Hart*

# Herbie

Herbie is a dachshund, you know the type I mean,
The strangest looking breed of dog you've surely ever seen,
With stubby legs and low-hung tummy, resting on the ground,
In every way, I have to say, a most peculiar hound!

His body is, well, rather long, you must admit it's true,
Perhaps it's simply that his little legs just never grew,
And though I love him dearly and I really mustn't tease,
He always gives the image that he's walking on his knees.

Though verti-cally challenged with horizontal stretch,
He never has a problem when I throw a ball with *"fetch!"*
Off into fields of golden wheat he charges nose-to-ground
And in the morning yet another corn circle is found.

Of being somewhat different, he never seems aware
And it is I who has to sigh when people stop and stare,
With cries of "look, a sausage dog!" and "what on earth is that?"
I wouldn't have this trouble if I'd settled for a cat.

But now the poem's over and I've finished with my jest,
I can tell you that my Herbie is in fact the very best -
He's beautiful, he's special and with him I'll never part
For he's found his place with me,
Both in my home and in my heart.

*Vicky Gifford*

# Ode To A Chocolate Labrador
## (Or my passion for chocolate)

Those big brown eyes that melt my heart
Your pretty face - sets you apart
My special girl, you're so much more
My darling precious Labrador.

You greet me with a bounding hug
When in the garden you have dug -
You're so excited I can see
To take me outside to the tree -
Where all the pansies used to sit
Now all remains is in a pit!

Into the pond you like to splash
The fish for shelter they do dash
Lilies all - out they come
You learnt to swim - not quite so dumb.

We have some fun, my girl and I
You laugh when I laugh, cry when I cry
My greatest friend - what are you worth?
You're my salvation, **salt of the earth.**

*Eileen Nicholls*

# Problems

Being a dog, I would like to say
About some problems, if I may
Regarding "Walkies", what must I do?
I'm very well trained, and wish to please you
I try not to wander where children play
I need to exercise every day
May I offer a plea from some of my friends
Please give us areas that are well signed,
In secluded places, where neighbours won't mind
It is wisely said, we are "Mans best friend"
So, please help us - not to offend.

*Patricia Denise*

# She

I never before knew such as she
That ball of furry love,
Such loyalty and comforting,
So frail yet lasting strength,
And I'm so glad I own her
Or is it I that am the slave.

They call her dog or sometimes bitch,
They treat her like a fool
And ban her from the marketplace,
They say she spreads diseases,
And I'm so glad I own her
Or is it I that am the slave.

Her life is all emotions show,
Of greeting when I return,
Of wagging tail and bounding yap,
Her contentment in my presence,
And I'm so glad I own her
Or is it I that am the slave.

*Richard Reeve*

# The Sickly Puppy

You were never a well little puppy,
When you should have yapped, you cried.
You were ill when just a tiny scrap
You very nearly died.
Yet, though so very small and young
You had the will to live;
We had the love to pull you through
We've so much more to give
So carry on recovering
For it won't be too late
Although you lost your puppyhood
Your future will be great!

*Elizabeth A. Brown*

# Watchdog

They say I'm not a 'watchdog'
But I really do my best
'Cos I'm watching all the time that I'm awake'
For I watch the television
And I watch while dinner's made
And I watch each single movement that they make.
I watch all the goings-on
When I'm lying out the front
And I watch the birds that fly up in the sky,
So before you're called a 'watchdog'
How much watching must you do?
And if it's REALLY worth it, tell me why.
Do you get a bigger dinner?
Do you get an extra bone?
Do you get more chocolate biscuits every day?
I've a feeling that you don't
So if it's all the same to you,
I'll be a 'watchdog' in my own sweet way!

*Alison Howells*

# A Pet Is For Life

It's Christmas time, presents to buy,
The children want a pet of their own,
So off you go into town, to see what you can find,
My brothers, sisters and me, we jump at the glass,
Barking and wagging our tails.

I see you pointing at me, I'm the one you want,
Next thing I know I am in a box,
You take me home, and you all make a fuss,
Christmas comes and goes, so does your love for me,
Gone are all my treats and walks,
No more attention, left in the cold,
Neglected, tied up soon forgotten,
Fed up, lonely, tired and hungry.

When will you come and feed me?
I am shivering from the cold,
Soon I am just skin and bones, when will it ever end,
Then one cold dark windy night,
I hear someone come for me, where are you taking me?
Where are we going too, please don't leave me.

I sit alone, not sure where I am,
I wander around, but I haven't much strength,
Is this the end, doesn't no one care?
Soon I see some lights, please hear my plight,
I collapse into a heap, I howl and cry,
Soon the door opens wide, you take me inside,
Soon you bathe an feed me, and heal my wounds,
Through lots of love and care, I soon recover,
This time it's for life not just for Christmas.

*H. Philp*

# Gaby

My little dog is sleeping
Beside me on the bed
All covered with her blanket
I can only see her head.

She's snoring very softly
Her little eyes shut tight
Her steady breathing soothes me
Through many a sleepless night.

Her little tummy rumbles
And she shuffles on the bed
Opens her eyes and wags her tail
So I stroke her furry head.

She stretches out her little legs
And gives a contented sigh
Then off she goes to sleep again
Knowing that I'm nearby.

And in the morning when it's light
And I open sleepy eyes
I see her friendly little face
Lying by my side.

*P. Vance*

# As We Walked Down The Leafy Lane

As the walk down the leafy lane,
My two black Labs and me,
There's so much nature going on,
So walk with us and see.

In springtime all new life adorns
Awake from its long sleep,
The cuckoo sings out merrily,
While the shepherd tends his sheep.

In summertime the sun is high.
The woodland dressed again,
A walk to view Gods garden,
Refreshed by bursts of rain.

It's autumn now the sun goes low,
Already scenes do change,
Hedgerows thick with berries red,
For birds, or to arrange.

It's wintertime with snow and ice,
The ground is now quite hard
You stop and look around awhile
The scenes portray a Christmas card.

*Shirley A. Chapman*

# Slush Puppies

Rufus waddles along like a fat little bear
The commands of his master are just wasted air,
He will sniff for an hour at one blade of grass
A dustcart drives by, he's a white lightening flash.

Misty, barks growls and whines like a wild feral beast
You think someone's losing an ankle at least.
The paperboy runs 'till he's quite out of breath.
When she catches him up she licks him to death.

They go by the title of West Highland White.
At bathtime, clean water gives them both a fright,
But the sight of a cow-pat or patch of black mud
Finds them rolling in bliss, yapping "Isn't this good".

*R. Guest*

# "Jonni" Just Can't Win

I'm fast asleep upon her chair,
I know it's not allowed.
People only?  That's not fair.
Us Cavaliers are proud.

Go for walkies; in the rain?
I hope you're only joking,
My sore paw's playing up again.
We don't both need a soaking.

A seaside paddle is more the mark
Those waves don't frighten me
You're sure that stick is not a shark?
I'm noted for my bravery.

I'm sure that I've been good today
I've tried my very best
I've walked to heel and didn't stray
And now I need a rest.

So I'm fast asleep upon "her" chair
She's going to wake me up.
And she will say, "No, no, not there:
You're a very naughty pup!".

*B. Knightley*

# I Can't....

So many cages,
So little time,
Will one of these dogs soon be mine?
Some noisy;
Some silent -
But all of them alone,
Each of them pleading -
"Take me home!"

Abandoned and injured,
Unwanted and disowned,
All they want is love and attention,
A basket,
A bone.

But you're not good with children,
You're destructive -
Can't you see,
I'm sorry,
I can't take you home -
You're new owner isn't me.

*Kirsty Nankeville*

# Tess

At home we have a puppy,
A little minx called Tess,
And although she's very lovable
She always makes a mess,
With her puddles on the carpet,
Little heaps on the floor,
Will she ever learn to sit and cry
To be let out the door?

The wallpaper beside her bed
Has a pattern all of its own
And the plaster that was underneath
Has mysteriously gone!
With artistic skill her scissor teeth
Make a collage on the floor
With a box of tissues, newspapers,
Old slippers, towels and more!

But although she's full of mischief,
We can't be cross for long,
For her friendly cheerful nature
Soon makes up for all the wrong.
We smile to see her sleeping
In her cosy basket curled
And we know we wouldn't swap her
For anything in the world!

*Susan Davies*

# Muffin's Ball

I'm SURE I left it somewhere in the hall!
My lovely, pink and squeaky, rubber ball.
I've searched high and I've searched low,
Where they've put it, I don't know!
It's not under the table or under the chair,
I've even looked under the cat, with long hair!

I managed to look in the airing cupboard;
For a minute or two, my hopes really soared.
A closer inspection found an old rubber glove -
And it WASN'T my toy, the ball, that I love!
It's not in the wardrobe, nor under the bed,
Might be in the garden, beneath the old shed.

I tried in the toy-box and in the bin,
Oh! Who! I wonder, committed this sin?
I MUST have my ball - without I'm sad,
Whoever has hid it, is making me mad!
I'm feeling real faint. Oh! What can I do?
I looked in the bath and behind our loo!

It's wicked! It's cruel! It shouldn't be done!
To stop a poor dog, from having her fun!
I've nothing to chase and nothing to worry,
I'll find out who did it, THEN they'll be sorry!
But wait! Just caught a whiff of pink, rubber ball,
It's high up above me and I'm not very tall.

I spy it LAST!  It's on the T.V.
How cruel life can be, to a wee dog like me!
I SEE IT!  IT'S THERE! - High up on the top,
Me, being a Cairn, I'll beg till I drop!
I WANT IT!  IT'S MINE!  My lovely pink ball!
NEXT time, I won't leave it, out in the hall!

*Joyce Dobson*

# Man's Best Friend

A dog is man's best friend they say,
How true,
When you're feeling sad and blue
She's there.
Always loving, always kind, a paw to give,
That's her.
A knowing look, that says to you
I'm here.
Never worry, never frown, though the world seems upside-down
Cheer up.
Life's for living, don't delay, play with me in a quiet way,
Have fun.
Soon your 'j'oi de vivre' returns
Because of her, take on the world,
It's yours.
The gentle unconditional love she gives, that lifts your spirit
And your heart, can only come,
FROM HER.

*Doreen McDonald Banks*

# Winning Ways

With your cute little face,
and the way your tail, you chase.
Add to this your mischief,
It becomes popular belief,
Our love is woven with lace.

Throughout the days,
We discover each other's ways.
During our hours of play,
You and I become firm friends,
For now and for always.

Now you have grown,
And the seed is sown,
For me to fall in love with you.
I give you a love, so very true,
A love, never before known.

Together in the twilight hours,
We sit side by side.
With me you constantly abide,
Together, forever and ever.
No other love is like ours.

From now on,
It is my dog and I.
Until eternity is nigh
I will enjoy his winning ways.
Our loneliness, is now gone.

*E. A. Stracey*

# The Chosen One

I took him from his loving mother,
From his father and his brother.
We left with memories and sighs
Of so sad looks of trusting eyes.

The journey home was filled with cries,
As we sped through the countryside.
The special one sent from above,
The chosen one for me to love.

His own small bed, his tiny pillow,
The chosen one - my puppy "Willow".

*Susan Jill Rostron*

# The Rover's Return

Pretty Molly rolled in myrtle.
Bert daresay'd she might be fertile.
Howard scorned. "Grey Bert, you've cracked.
Mol' just scratched am itchy back".
Bert declared old Howard dense.
Howard knocked Bert's lack of sense.

While the gaffers long debated,
Mol' danced out and procreated.

*Anne E. Tener*

# Grace

We brought her home on a sunny day
Eight weeks old, just wanting to play
We'd thought long and hard about getting a puppy
And now here she was, all soft and fluffy
But, were we too old?  Could we keep up the pace?
She was adorable, and we named her "Grace".

She was a bundle of fun and like all German Shepherds
Nothing grew evenly, it was all so haphazard -
Great lollopy paws, and a head far too small
For such a huge pair of ears, but that's not all,
With her whiplash tail, round the room she would race
Sending everything flying - who named her Grace?

Winter has come and she loves the snow
She "sings" at the door, eager to go
With a run and a jump into a drift
Something was there, it has to be sniffed
Then she slides into me, and while I'm flat on my face
Clambers all over me - who named her Grace?

Sitting relaxed in my nice comfy chair
She lies at my feet, and gives me the stare
That tells me there's something I've forgotten to do
We've had our last walk, she's expecting a chew
She knows where they're kept, she'll show me the place
As teacups get scattered, I wonder - who named her Grace?

She's three years old now, and an absolute pleasure
Who needs the lottery, she's my great treasure
She's developed and grown into a real beauty
And with a bow on her collar, she looks such a cutie
She loves training classes, but in the obstacle race
Wrecked the tunnel and hurdles - and I named her Grace.

*Pauline Southby*

# True Companion

A dog is yours wherever you are whether
the parting is long or short the joyful
welcome stays the same, he makes no criticism
of your ways, appearance never counts, he is
forever loyal and true.
Sad when you are, pleased when your
happiness shows through, a comfortable chair
the fireside, or country lane, it matters not
as long as he is with you, faithful until
life's journeys end, a dog is devotion plus.

## *Catherine Neale*